THE
CHRISTMAS
HOUR

Meditations for Advent, Christmas and Epiphany

Allan Smith

Published by: Bishop Sheen Today

www.bishopsheentoday.com

Title: The Christmas Hour. Meditations for Advent, Christmas and Epiphany.

Compiled by Allan J. Smith. Includes bibliographical references.

Identifiers: Paperback: 978-1-997627-93-7

eBook: 978-1-997627-94-4

Hardcover: 978-1-997627-95-1

Subjects: Christmas – Epiphany - Jesus Christ — Mary – Joseph – Shepherds – Magi – Holidays — Prayer – Meditation – Archbishop Fulton J. Sheen – Reflection

Front Cover Artwork: Antonio da Correggio (c.1518-1520) – Adoration of the Child. Public Domain, image courtesy Wikimedia Commons.

EPIGRAPH

*"And the Word became flesh
and dwelt among us."*

— John 1:14

Table of Contents

PART II
CHRISTMAS
Adoration. Wonder. The God Who Comes Small.

PART III
EPIPHANY
Revelation, Seeking, Guidance, Wonder

PART IV
MARY & JOSEPH
The Holy Home. Hidden Love. Ordinary Holiness.

PART V
THE BETHLEHEM WITHIN
The Birth of Christ in the Soul. Union. Love that lives.

PART VI
TREASURY OF CHRISTMAS MEDITATIONS
For Prayer and Reflection Throughout the Season

FOREWORD

There are seasons in the spiritual life when God invites us to step away from noise and hurry, and to enter the stillness where He speaks to the heart.

Christmas is one of those seasons.

The world celebrates loudly. It decorates, gathers, exchanges, prepares, and strives to create joy. Yet the mystery of Christmas did not begin in noise or spectacle. It began in silence. In a hidden place. Under starlight. In the quiet embrace of a Mother who held God close.

What took place in Bethlehem was more than an event in history. It was the nearness of God — the moment when the Eternal stepped into time, when heaven bent low to touch the earth, when love took on a face we could see and a heart that could be loved.

Christ came quietly then, and He comes quietly now.

The meditations that follow are meant to create space for that quiet coming — a manger within the soul. They are not meant to be rushed through or consumed, but received slowly, prayerfully, gently.

A single meditation may be enough for a day. A single line may be enough for a moment of prayer. A single silence may be enough for Christ to enter.

May these reflections help us to notice the humble ways God approaches us:

in silence that calls us to listen,
in poverty that teaches us to let go,
in love that invites us to surrender.

And may the Child who once found room in Bethlehem
find room also in us.

Come, Lord Jesus.
Be born in us again.

PART I

ADVENT
The Longing, The Listening,
The Preparing

"Prepare the way of the Lord."

— Isaiah 40:3

INTRODUCTION

There are seasons in the spiritual life when God seems silent, and yet, it is in this silence that He prepares hearts for His coming. Advent is not merely a time on the calendar — it is the deep and ancient cry of humanity waiting for God. Every longing, every restlessness, every hope that will not go away is Advent at work within us. We wait not for an idea, but for a Person. We wait not for comfort, but for **Love made flesh**.

The world waited for centuries for the Messiah. Yet even now, Christ waits for us — waits to be welcomed, to be given room, to be born again not in a stable of wood, but in the chambers of the human heart. Advent teaches us to slow down, to listen with the ears of the soul, and to prepare a place that hunger alone cannot fill.

We begin here — in the ache, the longing, the holy desire because the one who truly waits, will truly see Him when He comes.

Advent is a time to slow down and make room for God.

We wait, not with worry, but with hope.

We listen for His voice in the quiet moments of the day.

We prepare our hearts, knowing He is near.

We cannot hurry the coming of Christ.

We can only welcome Him when He arrives.

So we clear a space within us

and let silence open the door.

In this season, we learn to wait with love.

The Meaning of the Christmas Hour

Christmas is not merely a date on the calendar or a memory of something long ago — it is the moment when **Heaven bent low to touch the earth.**

God entered time so that time itself could become holy.

We often rush through life as though everything depends on us — our effort, our strength, our planning. But Christmas reminds us that salvation does not begin with what **we** do, but with what **God** has done.

He came quietly — not in power, but in poverty.
Not demanding love, but offering it.
Not overwhelming us, but inviting us.

Christmas is an hour of **stillness**, when God knocks gently at the door of our hearts.

And it is an hour of **decision** — whether we will make room for Him.

May we find His presence today, even in the places we least expect.

Lord Jesus, grant me the grace to love You more today than yesterday, and more tomorrow than today.

Amen.

The Waiting of the World

Before Christ came, humanity waited — sometimes knowingly, sometimes unknowingly — for Someone who could restore what was broken.

We still feel that longing today.
We long for peace.
We long for healing.
We long for meaning.

And into that longing, God comes.
Not to remove our hunger, but to **fill it with Himself.**

Waiting is not a failure of faith.
Waiting is the posture of the heart that trusts God's timing.

The manger teaches us that **God arrives at the right moment** — not early, not late, but when love is ready to be received.

May we find His presence today, even in the places we least expect.

Lord Jesus, grant me the grace to love You more today than yesterday, and more tomorrow than today.

Amen.

Preparing a Place

There was no room for Him at the inn — and so He chose a manger.

Not because He was unworthy of a palace, but because **He wanted to dwell where hearts are humble.**

The greatest preparation for Christmas is not our decorations, our gatherings, or our plans — it is the opening of our hearts.

Christ does not demand perfection before He enters.
He asks only for **welcome.**

Every time we choose forgiveness over resentment, generosity over self-preservation, and trust over fear — we make room for Him.

He does not need a palace.
He needs a heart that is willing.

May we find His presence today, even in the places we least expect.

Lord Jesus, grant me the grace to love You more today than yesterday, and more tomorrow than today.

Amen.

God Comes in Silence

———————

The great works of God often begin quietly.

The world expected thunder and armies, but God came in stillness — in a crib, in a cave, under starlight.

Silence is not empty.

It is where God speaks.

If we do not hear Him, it may be because our lives are filled with too many voices — too many demands, too much noise of self, anxiety, and hurry.

Christmas invites us to **enter silence** — not escape from life, but return to the One who gives life meaning.

He comes gently — and waits to be welcomed.

May we find His presence today, even in the places we least expect.

Lord Jesus, grant me the grace to love You more today than yesterday, and more tomorrow than today.

Amen.

The God Who Knocks

God never forces His way into the human heart.

He **knocks** — patiently, respectfully, lovingly.

He stands at the door of our freedom, waiting for us to open.

Christmas is not only the story of God coming into the world — it is the story of whether the world receives Him.

Every day, He approaches in moments of compassion, in unexpected beauty, in the stirring of conscience, in the quiet longing for something more.

He asks only for **welcome**.

May we find His presence today, even in the places we least expect.

Lord Jesus, grant me the grace to love You more today than yesterday, and more tomorrow than today.

Amen.

The Silence of Bethlehem

The night Christ was born was not loud with triumph — it was quiet.

No trumpets, no crowds, no announcements across the earth.

Only the soft breathing of animals, the whisper of straw, the stillness of night.

God came in silence so that **we would learn where to listen**.

The deepest things in life are spoken quietly —
love, sorrow, beauty, repentance, longing.

If we want to find God, we must make room for silence.

Not the silence of emptiness, but the silence of **attention** —
the silence that listens for God's footsteps.

Bethlehem teaches us that God does not shout.
He waits for the heart that is still enough to hear Him.

May we find His presence today, even in the places we least expect.

Lord Jesus, grant me the grace to love You more today than yesterday, and more tomorrow than today.

Amen.

The Inn and the Manger

———————

There was no room in the inn — but there was room in the manger.

The inn was crowded, busy, filled with noise, movement, distraction.

The manger was quiet, poor, forgotten — but open.

The heart can be like either place.

Sometimes we fill our lives so completely — with plans, anxieties, possessions, and noise —
that there is no room for God.

Yet He never forces His way in.
He looks for the open space, however humble.

The place where Christ is born is not the place of perfection, but the place of **welcome**.

If we offer Him even a small space of silence, of kindness, of prayer, of surrender,
He will fill it with Himself.

May we find His presence today, even in the places we least expect.

Lord Jesus, grant me the grace to love You more today than yesterday, and more tomorrow than today.

Amen.

Are We All Innkeepers?

———————

Every soul is an inn, and Christ comes again and again, seeking room.

Sometimes we refuse Him because we are busy.
Sometimes because we are comfortable.
Sometimes because we fear what His presence might change.

To welcome Christ is to allow other guests to depart —
pride, resentment, greed, bitterness, self-reliance.

Christ does not enter by force.
He waits at the door of the heart.

The question of Christmas is not:
Was there room in Bethlehem?

But:
Is there room in me?

May we find His presence today, even in the places we least expect.

Lord Jesus, grant me the grace to love You more today than yesterday, and more tomorrow than today.

Amen.

The Paradise God Prepared

Before God created Adam, He prepared a garden — a paradise of beauty.

Before God came to us in the flesh, He prepared **Mary** — a paradise of grace.

She is the living sanctuary,
the garden where the new Adam would walk,
the dwelling where God would take on our humanity.

Mary is not distant or unreachable.
She is the place where love learned to beat with a human heart.

To welcome Mary is to draw near to Christ,
just as He drew near to us through her.

She does not replace Him.
She reveals Him.

May we find His presence today, even in the places we least expect.

Lord Jesus, grant me the grace to love You more today than yesterday, and more tomorrow than today.

Amen.

God in the Unexpected Places

We often assume that God must reveal Himself in ways that are grand, obvious, and unmistakable — in palaces, in power, in things the world calls impressive. Yet the story of Bethlehem teaches us something different. When the Saviour came, He was not welcomed in the inn, the place of comfort and importance. He was born instead in a stable — a place of simplicity, humility, and quiet.

God chose to step into the world where few were looking for Him.

The One who lit the stars came into a world where He needed the warmth of the animals beside Him. The Creator entered creation so small that His hands could not yet reach for His mother's face. The Eternal Word came in silence. The Almighty came in weakness.

Why would God come this way?

So that no one could say,

"God is too far from me."

He comes to the humble so the humble may find Him.

He comes to the poor so the poor may not feel forgotten.

He comes quietly so the restless and weary can approach without fear.

If we look only for God in the spectacular, we may miss Him.

But if we seek Him in the simple, the hidden, the ordinary —
we will find Him.

Prayer

*Lord Jesus, open my eyes to recognize Your presence in the quiet and
unexpected places of my life. May I never overlook You because I expected
You to come differently. Come to me in humility, and teach my heart to
welcome You.*

Amen.

When God Prepares Something Beautiful

Before God does anything great, He prepares.

Before the first man took his first breath, the world was shaped with wonder: oceans filled with life, skies crossed with birds, fields clothed in green, rivers winding through gold-touched soil. Beauty came first, so that when man opened his eyes, he would awaken to the goodness of God.

Creation itself was a love-letter prepared in advance.

And when the time came for God to enter His own creation—not merely as its Maker, but as its Child—He prepared again.

But this time, the preparation was not a garden.

It was **a heart**.

A heart made ready long before Bethlehem.

A heart capable of receiving, nurturing, and loving the very Life of God.

A new Eden—not of trees and rivers, but of faith, humility, and grace.

When God desires to dwell somewhere, He prepares the place with care.

This is not only true of Eden.
Not only true of Mary.
It is true of **us**.

Christ longs to make His home in the soul.
But He does not force the door.
He waits for us to let Him prepare the inner garden:
to clear away what chokes life,
to uproot what wounds love,
to plant what bears eternal fruit.

The God of Genesis is still at work.
Still creating.
Still preparing.
Still breathing life.

If we allow Him, our hearts may yet become a paradise of His presence.

May we let Him make us new.

May we find His presence today, even in the places we least expect.

The King Who Comes in Silence

_____

There is something in the human heart that longs to bow.
Even in a world that claims to love equality,
we still seek someone to lift above ourselves.

We crown athletes, movie stars, singers, leaders.
We call them *kings* and *queens* —
not because we think they are divine,
but because something in us remembers
that we were made to reverence greatness.

We are never so small as when we live only for ourselves.

We are never so great as when we stand before the Truly Great.

And so humanity has always searched for a King.

But the King we were made for does not sit on a jeweled throne.

He does not wear gold, or summon armies,
or command fear.

The true King came to us as a Child.
His throne was a manger.
His first crown was straw.
His first subjects were shepherds who smelled of fields and night.

The question still echoes across the centuries:
"Where is He who is born King?"

Not in the palaces of the powerful.
Not in the noise of crowds.
Not in the displays of prestige or success.

But in the quiet.
In the hidden places.
In the hearts that make room.

We find Him where love is simple.
Where humility is chosen.
Where we kneel.

For Christ is the King who does not force our allegiance…
He waits for our adoration.

May we find His presence today,
even in the places we least expect.

The King We Were Made to Find

———————

Even those who claim to reject kings
cannot escape the longing to admire, to exalt, to adore.

We crown celebrities, praise leaders, honor champions —
because the heart knows it was made
to bow before greatness.

But the true King does not appear in splendor or force.
He comes in humility, in gentleness, in silence.

His throne is a manger.
His crown is love.

To find Him, we must go where the proud do not go —
to the quiet places where the humble adore.

There, the heart knows its King.

The Door of the Heart

———————

There are many who know the story of Bethlehem well. They can describe the star, the manger, the shepherds, even the royal Magi who traveled far from the East. But knowing the *story* of Bethlehem is not the same as welcoming the Child who was born there. The difference lies in the heart — whether it is open, or full, or shut.

We remember the innkeeper in the Gospel narrative, the one who turned Mary and Joseph away because there was "no room." Perhaps he was overwhelmed by the crowds, the noise, the demands of the day. Perhaps he judged by appearances — seeing only poverty and inconvenience at his door. Whatever his reason, the result was the same: the Christ Child found no welcome under his roof.

And so the question becomes personal: **Are we all innkeepers?**

It is one thing to know about Christ — to know the Scriptures, the history, the meaning of Christmas — and another to welcome Him within. Herod knew the prophecies too, yet his heart responded with fear and resistance. Knowledge alone is not love. The shepherds, unlearned and poor, opened their hearts. They made room. They went to the manger with haste.

Every soul has a door. Every heart has a room. And every person, at some moment, stands where the innkeeper stood — deciding whether to let Christ in.

The Child of Bethlehem does not enter by force. He does not break down the door. He knocks quietly, gently, waiting for us to make space. But to receive Him is to let go of the "other guests" we have allowed to settle comfortably in our hearts — pride, resentment, greed, distraction, self-reliance, comfort without sacrifice. Christ's presence reshapes the interior life. He clears, purifies, reorders, heals. And that is why His coming can feel costly.

Yet what He asks us to surrender is so small compared to what He gives. We give up the spark, and He gives the flame. We open one small room, and He fills the house with light.

To say "yes" to Christ today is to become Bethlehem — a place where God may be born anew. It is to allow love to enter where fear once lived, peace where restlessness once ruled, and gentleness where hardness once held ground.

The door of the heart opens from the inside.
And Christ is still knocking.

PART II

CHRISTMAS
Adoration. Wonder.
The God Who Comes Small.

*"She gave birth to her firstborn son
and laid Him in a manger."*

— Luke 2:7

INTRODUCTION

The mystery of Christmas is not simply that God came to us, but that He came **small**. Heaven bent low; Infinity became an Infant. In the stillness of Bethlehem, Love took on a face. The God whom the universe cannot contain allowed Himself to be held in the arms of a mother. The Eternal Word did not thunder from the heavens — He **cooed**.

Christmas asks us to believe that the Almighty hides Himself in littleness, tenderness, and silence. The God of angelic choirs now sleeps in straw. The One who formed galaxies now curls His fingers around Mary's hand. The world did not recognize Him — but the humble did.

To celebrate Christmas rightly is to kneel.

Christmas is the moment when God draws near.

Not in power, but in gentleness.

Not in glory, but in a Child.

We do not need to understand everything — we only need to come close.

We kneel before the manger, not to figure out God, but to love Him.

This is the season of **receiving**.

We open our hearts the way Mary opened her arms.

We welcome Christ the way Joseph welcomed mystery.

Let us draw close to the Child,
and let love be simple again.

The Poverty of the Manger

———————

Christ was born in poverty — not because God romanticizes hardship, but because **He wanted nothing to stand between Him and the human heart.**

If He had come in splendor, the proud would have claimed Him.

If He had come in power, the strong would have gathered around Him.

But He came in humility, so that **all might draw near.**

The manger teaches us that God does not wait for perfect conditions before He enters our lives.

He comes into whatever is real — whatever is ordinary — whatever is small.

He sanctifies what the world overlooks.

The place where Christ is welcomed becomes holy.

May we find His presence today, even in the places we least expect.

Lord Jesus, grant me the grace to love You more today than yesterday, and more tomorrow than today.

Amen.

The Shepherd's Awakening

The shepherds were not scholars or rulers or elites.

They were ordinary people keeping watch in the quiet of night.

But it was **to them** that Heaven opened.

Why?
Because their hearts were awake.
Because they were attentive.
Because silence had prepared them to hear God.

God often comes to us in moments that seem small —
a whisper of conscience, a moment of beauty, an unexpected
stirring of hope.

To notice Him, we do not need brilliance.
We need **openness**.

The shepherds teach us how to receive Christmas:
not with analysis, but with wonder.

May we find His presence today, even in the places we least expect.

*Lord Jesus, grant me the grace to love You more today than yesterday, and
more tomorrow than today.*

Amen.

The Wonder of the Child

The infinite God became a child.

Not because He needed to, but because **we needed Him to**.

A child disarms us.
A child does not intimidate or overwhelm.
A child invites tenderness, affection, gentleness, love.

God knows the human heart.

He knows that love grows easiest where there is humility and trust.

So He came small.

So that we would not be afraid.

So that we would learn that **God is love**, and love is never proud.

The manger is not just a scene — it is a message:
Come close. Do not fear. I am yours.

May we find His presence today, even in the places we least expect.

Lord Jesus, grant me the grace to love You more today than yesterday, and more tomorrow than today.

Amen.

The Joy That Cannot Be Taken

———————

The joy of Christmas is not temporary, like celebration or excitement.

It is deeper — quiet, steady, rooted in **God-with-us**.

This joy does not depend on circumstances.
It does not fade when life becomes difficult.
It does not disappear when feelings shift.

It remains, because it comes from the One who remains.

Joy is not what we feel — joy is *Who* we have.

And we have Christ.

If He is with us, then even in sorrow there can be peace,
and even in hardship there can be hope.

This is the joy the world cannot take.

May we find His presence today, even in the places we least expect.

Lord Jesus, grant me the grace to love You more today than yesterday, and more tomorrow than today.

Amen.

The Infinity of Littleness

We discover greatness only when we become small.

A child sees everything as large — because the child is small.

So too in the spiritual life:
The humble discover the greatness of God.

Christ came as a child to teach us that the door to God is low, and only those who **bend** can enter.

Humility is not weakness — it is clarity.

It allows us to see reality — ourselves, others, God — as they truly are.

To be small before God is to be open to wonder, awe, and love.

May we find His presence today, even in the places we least expect.

Lord Jesus, grant me the grace to love You more today than yesterday, and more tomorrow than today.

Amen.

Christmas Is for the Broken

———————

Christ did not come for those who believe themselves good enough.

He came for those who know they need mercy.

Christmas is not the feast of the perfect —
it is the feast of the hopeful.

The manger is not surrounded by the proud,
but by shepherds, wanderers, and seekers.

God is drawn to the humble heart,
the heart that says:
Lord, I need You.

The joy of Christmas begins where self-reliance ends.

May we find His presence today, even in the places we least expect.

Lord Jesus, grant me the grace to love You more today than yesterday, and more tomorrow than today.

Amen.

The Child We Must Remember

The world has always searched for peace — through wealth, through progress, through power, through knowledge.

Yet peace is not something we build — it is Someone we welcome.

Chesterton imagined three modern wise men bringing gifts of technology, control, and force — only to be told that they had forgotten **the Child**.

We too can forget Him — even while doing many good things.

Peace is not found in the greatness of our hands,
but in the humility of our hearts.

To remember the Child is to remember who we are
and who we belong to.

May we find His presence today, even in the places we least expect.

Lord Jesus, grant me the grace to love You more today than yesterday, and more tomorrow than today.

Amen.

The Humility That Sees the Child

The proud man cannot recognize God in the manger.
He looks for kings in palaces, not in straw.
He expects wisdom to arrive with applause, not with silence.

But God hides Himself in littleness
so that only the humble will find Him.

To enter Bethlehem, one must **stoop**.
To recognize Christ, one must **kneel**.

The one who bows discovers that the cave is not darkness —
but the doorway into light.

Christmas teaches us that God does not ask us to be great —
only to be small enough to receive Him.

May we find His presence today, even in the places we least expect.

Lord Jesus, grant me the grace to love You more today than yesterday, and more tomorrow than today.

Amen.

Where Love and Child Are One

In most births, love rises from earth to heaven.

Human love reaches upward and asks for blessing.

But at Christmas, **love came down**.

The Child of Bethlehem was not simply the result of human longing — He was the answer to it.

Mary did not stumble into motherhood.
She **willed** it in love:
"Let it be done unto me according to Your word."

Her motherhood began not in her body, but in her **heart**.

And the Child she bore was not merely hers —
He was **God's love made visible**.

Where love is pure and surrendered,
God makes Himself known.

In the manger,
Love and Child are one.

May we find His presence today, even in the places we least expect.

Lord Jesus, grant me the grace to love You more today than yesterday, and more tomorrow than today.

Amen.

The Mother Resembles the Child

———————

When a child is born, we ask,
"Whom does the baby resemble?"

But at Christmas, it is different.

Christ did not come to imitate Mary.
Mary was formed to reflect **Him**.

Her purity, her tenderness, her humility —
these were not merely her own virtues,
but the radiance of the One she carried.

She held Him in her arms,
but she was the one being shaped.

Most mothers look up to heaven.
Mary looked **down** —
for Heaven was in her arms.

To love Mary is simply to learn how to love Jesus
as she loved Him.

May we find His presence today, even in the places we least expect.

Lord Jesus, grant me the grace to love You more today than yesterday, and more tomorrow than today.

Amen.

Why We Give Gifts at Christmas

We give gifts because **God first gave Himself.**

Love always desires to give.
And the greatest gift is presence —
to say with our actions:
"You matter. You are loved."

Every small gift at Christmas
is a reflection of the Gift in the manger —
God become man,
so that humanity may become like God.

May we find His presence today, even in the places we least expect.

Lord Jesus, grant me the grace to love You more today than yesterday, and more tomorrow than today.

Amen.

Fear Not — Joy Has Drawn Near

When the angels appeared to the shepherds, their first response was fear. And we understand why — when the human heart encounters the Holy, something in us trembles. We recognize how small we are. We feel the weight of our sins, our worries, our limitations. The shepherds were ordinary men, living hidden lives. Yet it was *to them* that heaven first announced the birth of the Saviour.

The message was simple, and it is spoken to us again today:

"Do not be afraid."

God does not come to overwhelm or frighten us.

He comes to reassure, comfort, and renew us.

The joy of Christmas is not the joy of noise, excitement, or distraction. It is the deeper joy that follows the lifting of a burden. The birth of Christ is the sign that the distance between God and humanity has been bridged. Heaven has drawn near. Peace is no longer something we reach for — it is Someone who has come to be with us.

The angels sing not because life is suddenly easy, but because God is *now with us* in it.

If there are anxieties, sorrows, or struggles in your life this season, do not rush past them. Bring them to the manger. Let the Christ Child place His hand upon your heart.

For where Christ is welcomed, **fear dissolves and joy begins.**

Prayer

Lord Jesus,
You know the worries I carry and the fears that weigh upon my heart.
Speak to me the same words the angels spoke: **Do not be afraid.**
Let Your presence bring peace to my soul
and lead me from fear into joy.
Be born in me, that I may live in Your peace.

Amen.

Christmas Is Not for "Nice" People

The Child born in Bethlehem was given a name: **Jesus**, which means *Savior.*

And a Savior is someone who comes to rescue, to lift up, to heal, to forgive.

Christmas, therefore, is not a feast for those who think they have no need of saving.

Christmas is **not** for the "nice,"
for those convinced of their own goodness,
for those content, polished, and satisfied.

It is for the *poor*, the *wounded*, the *restless*, the *hungry of heart.*
It is for those who know they need mercy.

The manger was not filled because it was beautiful—
but because it was **empty**.

So too, the soul that admits its emptiness discovers room for God.

Those whom Christ welcomed were not the admired but the ashamed;
not the flawless but the flawed.

The lost sheep is gathered home while the ninety–nine stand aside.

The lost coin becomes the occasion of rejoicing.

He chose to sit at table with sinners,
to love those others avoided,
to lift those others dismissed.

And perhaps the greatest surprise of Heaven
will not be who *got in*—
but that **we ourselves were welcomed**.

For God did not come because we were good.
He came because we were **loved**.

Christmas is not for the "nice."
Christmas is for the *real*, the *broken*, the *convertible*,
those willing to be found.

When Christmas Happens Within Us

————————

What does it matter if Christ was born in Bethlehem two
thousand years ago,
if He is not also born in us?

The Child in the manger is not merely a memory of the past —
He is a **gift meant to be received in the present**.
Christ is the pattern, and we are the coin meant to bear His
image.

The first Christmas happened in history,
but the **second Christmas** happens in the soul.

Everything in creation rises by being taken up into something
greater.

The plant draws the mineral into itself.
The animal raises up plant life into higher life.
The human person gathers chemical, plant, and animal life
into a being capable of love, sacrifice, and eternity.

And so God came down—
not to remain below,
but to **lift us up** into His divine life.

But He will not force Himself.
Just as He waited for Mary's free yes,
He waits for ours.

If Christ came today with the remedy for the sickness of sin,
how tragic it would be to simply admire Him,
yet refuse the cure.

Christmas is meant to be *received*.
Not merely remembered.

It is not just wonderful that *God came to us.*
The deeper wonder is that **we are allowed to go to Him**.

A moment of turning toward Him,
a whispered prayer of surrender,
a quiet offering of our heart
—this is where **Christmas becomes real**.

Christ is not only born in Bethlehem.
Christ is born in the soul that welcomes Him.

Remember the Child

———————

The world has always searched for peace. Every age has produced its thinkers, its movements, its philosophies, its plans for a new and better world. And yet, with all our progress, we still find ourselves restless. Still aching. Still longing.

Archbishop Fulton J. Sheen recalls a story from G. K. Chesterton about *three modern wise men*. They were seekers — not of truth, but of solutions.

The first brought **wealth**, believing that affluence could heal the human heart.

The second brought **science**, confident that control over nature would bring harmony.

The third brought **power**, even the power to destroy, imagining that fear could ensure peace.

They came to the city of Peace and found Joseph standing at its gate. They presented their gifts, their achievements, their strategies — and they were turned away.

"What else could possibly be needed?" they asked.

Joseph whispered to each one:
You have forgotten the Child.

In every generation, the world repeats this mistake.

We try to build peace without innocence, without humility, without surrender, without God. We seek progress without adoration. We want the Kingdom, but not the King.

But peace is not something we invent.
Peace is Someone we welcome.

The Wise Men of Bethlehem knew peace because they knelt before Christ.

The world loses peace whenever it forgets Him.

So the invitation of Advent is simple:

Remember the Child.
Seek Him.
Welcome Him.
Adore Him.

Peace will follow.

May we find His presence today, even in the places we least expect.

Before the Manger

_____

When we come before the manger, something in us becomes still.

Not because the scene is sentimental or quaint, but because we are standing before a love so pure that it reveals the truth about us. In the presence of Christ and His Mother, our souls remember what they were made for.

Mary does not draw attention to herself in that moment. Her beauty is not the beauty of outward form, but of a heart entirely given to God — a heart transparent with grace. Her purity does not make us feel small, but seen. It is not a purity that excludes — it welcomes, it invites, it heals.

To stand before the manger is to recognize two things at once:

God is more loving than we imagined.
And we are more in need of His love than we admit.

This is not a humiliation; it is an awakening.

Christmas is not simply the memory of a holy night long ago. It is the realization that God comes _still_:
to the humble,
to the searching,
to the weary,
to those who know they cannot save themselves.

The Child in the crib speaks not with words, but with presence:

"You are loved.
You are not forgotten.
You are worth coming for."

And so we kneel — not because we are perfect, but because we are called.

May we carry this awareness gently today:
God comes close to the places we would rather hide.
He chooses to dwell where we need Him most.

May we find His presence today, even in the places we least expect.

The New Melody of Christmas

Before there was music on earth, there was music in God — a harmony that filled creation with beauty and order. Every creature was meant to play its part in this symphony of love.

But when the human heart turned away, the music broke. A discord entered the world — a note of pride, of self, of separation. And once the harmony was wounded, humanity could not restore it by itself.

So God began a new song.

Not with power. Not with command.
But with a Child.

The first note of the new melody was a cry in Bethlehem — soft, small, and pure. In that Child, God wrote a new beginning. A new humanity. A new way of loving.

Those who join their lives to His become part of that music — no longer "once-born," but "twice-born,"
no longer alone, but taken up into the great harmony of Christ.

Christmas is the invitation to let our discord become part of His song — to let grace rewrite what sin has damaged,
to let mercy soften what pride has hardened,
to let Christ tune our hearts again.

Every yes to Him becomes a note in the new melody of love.

May we find His presence today, even in the places we least expect.

The Wood of the Manger, the Wood of the Cross

———————

It is sometimes easier to understand the love of the Cross
than the love of the Cradle.

We can grasp the idea of sacrifice —
a life given out of love.
But the humility of *infancy*,
the Almighty choosing weakness,
silence, and helplessness —
this is a mystery that quiets the soul.

He accepted the manger
because there was no room for Him in the inn.
He accepted the Cross
because hearts had closed themselves to Him.

Disowned when He entered His own creation,
rejected as He left it.

A stranger's stable welcomed Him at His birth.
A stranger's tomb received Him at His death.
He lay between an ox and an ass at Bethlehem,
and between two thieves at Calvary.

The swaddling bands of His infancy
would one day become the cloths of His burial.

His life was not simply a path *toward* the Cross.
The Cross was there from the beginning.

Its shadow fell backward
over every moment of His earthly life.

We go from the known into the unknown —
stumbling, learning, losing, hoping.
But He went from the known to the known:
from the purpose of His coming
to the fulfillment of it.

There was no tragedy in His life.
There was love — chosen, deliberate, enduring.

The manger is the Cross in miniature.
The Cross is the manger lifted high.

And for those of us who know ourselves
to be like stables —
untidy inside, carrying burdens,
housing the "beasts" of our own weakness —
there is great consolation:

He does not fear such a dwelling.
He chooses it.

And when He enters,
joy becomes possible again.
Joy that whispers in the soul:

Merry Christmas.
Merry Christmas.

How Low Love Can Bend

––––––––––

Imagine lowering yourself to the level
of a creature far beneath you.

This is only a faint comparison
to the humility of God becoming man.

The manger leads to the Cross —
the love that bends low
is the love that gives all.

Christmas is not sentiment —
it is sacrifice.

May we find His presence today, even in the places we least expect.

Lord Jesus, grant me the grace to love You more today than yesterday, and more tomorrow than today.

Amen.

Because He First Gave Himself

————————

Christmas is the feast of giving.

For most of the year, we are busy *acquiring* — gathering, earning, arranging, protecting, holding.

But at Christmas, something softens. The heart enlarges. We remember that joy is found not in what we possess, but in what we **share**.

Why do we give gifts at Christmas?

Because we were given **a Gift**.

God did not send us a message, or a symbol, or a reminder — He gave **Himself**.

The Eternal stepped into time.
The Creator entered His own creation.
The Artist came into His own studio — not as a visitor, but as a Child placed into human arms.

His glory was veiled in the simplicity of ordinary flesh.
The One who hung the stars knew hunger, cold, tears, and weariness.

Never again could we say,
"God does not understand my suffering."

Never again could we claim that love is too costly,
for Love has already paid the highest price.

51

So when we give at Christmas —
when we wrap a gift without calculating its worth,
when we offer kindness without counting the cost —
we are imitating Him.

The Gift that was given in Bethlehem
has no price tag.
It cannot be bought.
It can only be **received**.

And once received — it longs to be given again.

May our giving this Christmas not be measured in ribbons or
paper,
but in love.

The Gift That Teaches Us to Give

We give gifts at Christmas
because we have first **received a Gift**.

God gave Himself to us —
not in power,
but in tenderness;
not in majesty,
but in vulnerability.

This Gift came wrapped in swaddling clothes
and laid in a manger.

Love always gives.
And so we give.

Not to match the greatness of His Gift —
for that is impossible —
but to let love overflow from the heart.

Every true gift is an echo of Bethlehem.

Let your giving be love —
not price, not performance, not obligation —
but love.

Discovering God at Christmas
by Archbishop Fulton J. Sheen

———————

There were only two classes of people who heard the cry Christmas night: shepherds and wise men.

Shepherds: those who know they know nothing.

Wise men: those who know they do not know everything.

Only the very simple and very learned discovered God — never the man with one book.

PART III

EPIPHANY

Revelation, Seeking, Guidance, Wonder

*"We have seen His star in the East
and have come to worship Him."*

— Matthew 2:2

INTRODUCTION

There comes a time in the spiritual life when Christ, once welcomed, begins to **reveal Himself**. This is Epiphany.

The hidden God becomes the guiding Light. The Wise Men journeyed not because they understood, but because they **trusted the star**. Epiphany teaches us that faith often walks by a light that others cannot see.

To follow Christ is to move — to leave behind what is familiar, to seek the Child wherever He leads. He may lead us through deserts, through questions, through quiet search. But He always leads us to Himself.

Here, we learn to become seekers.

Epiphany teaches us that God can be found by those who seek Him.

He calls us forward, one step at a time.

The Wise Men did not know the whole path.

They simply followed the light they were given.

So it is with us.

We may not see the full way ahead.

But we can follow the small light of faith.

We can take the next step.

God will lead us to Christ
if we keep our hearts open and willing.

The Journey of the Wise Men

The Wise Men travelled far — not guided by certainty, but by **trust.**

They followed a light in the sky because they sensed a greater light waiting at its end.

They remind us that faith is a **journey**, not a possession.

We do not always see the destination clearly.

We take one step, then another.

The Wise Men did not find Christ in the palace where logic led them —
but in the humble place where **God** led them.

Our path to God may not look like we imagined.

But if we keep seeking, we will find Him —
not always where we expect, but always where we need.

May we find His presence today, even in the places we least expect.

Lord Jesus, grant me the grace to love You more today than yesterday, and more tomorrow than today.

Amen.

The Light in the Darkness

———————

The world into which Christ was born was not peaceful or pure.
It was weary, fractured, longing.

He did not wait for the world to become worthy —
He came **into its darkness** to bring the light.

Light does not ask the darkness for permission.
It does not negotiate.
It simply shines — and the darkness cannot overcome it.

There are places within us that still long for that light:

- our fears
- our hidden wounds
- our unanswered questions
- our hopes waiting to wake again

Christ enters those places gently.

We do not have to remove the darkness first.
We only need to open the door.

May we find His presence today, even in the places we least expect.

Lord Jesus, grant me the grace to love You more today than yesterday, and more tomorrow than today.

Amen.

The Light That Enters the Cave

Archbishop Fulton Sheen reminds us that the Light of Christ
does not frighten the humble —
only the proud.

The shepherds were not afraid to draw near.
They knew their need.
They went to the cave as beggars and returned as men reborn.

But others feared the Light.
Herod feared losing power.
The innkeeper feared discomfort.
The comfortable feared change.

The Light of Christ reveals — but it also heals.
It uncovers — but it also restores.

If we allow the Light to touch even the hidden places,
we will not shrink — we will shine.

May we find His presence today, even in the places we least expect.

*Lord Jesus, grant me the grace to love You more today than yesterday, and
more tomorrow than today.*

Amen.

The Humble and the Wise

Those who came to the manger were not the proud, nor the self-sufficient.

It was the **shepherds** and the **wise men**:

- The shepherds came because they *knew they knew nothing.*
- The wise men came because they *knew they did not know everything.*

Both possessed **humility** — and humility opened the door to adoration.

Pride stands outside the stable and evaluates.
Humility kneels inside and worships.

Christmas is not found in learning, status, refinement, or intellect.
It is found in the soul that knows its need.

To kneel before the Christ Child is not to shrink —
it is to stand in truth.

May we find His presence today, even in the places we least expect.

Lord Jesus, grant me the grace to love You more today than yesterday, and more tomorrow than today.

Amen.

The First Note in a New Symphony

God created the world in harmony — a perfect symphony of love and order.

But humanity chose a different note — a discord born of pride.
And like a sound that echoes endlessly,
that disharmony spread through history.

Yet God did not abandon His work.
He began **a new composition**.

And the first note of this new song
was the cry of a Child in Bethlehem.

A melody of mercy.
A harmony of peace.
A music that invites all people
to return to love.

When we unite our lives to Him,
our broken notes are gathered
into His beautiful song.

May our hearts be tuned to His.

May we find His presence today, even in the places we least expect.

Lord Jesus, grant me the grace to love You more today than yesterday, and more tomorrow than today.

Amen.

The Light We Reflect

There is a beautiful order in God's creation: the sun shines with its own light, and the moon reflects that light to the earth. So it is in the spiritual life. Christ is the source of all grace, and Mary is the perfect reflection of that grace.

Mary does not draw attention to herself. She does not speak of her own greatness. She simply receives the love of God, and in receiving it, she shines. When we look to her, we see what happens when a human heart makes room for God without hesitation, without fear, without reserve.

There are seasons in our lives when the world feels like night — when light is dim and direction is uncertain. During those times, Christ is still shining, though our eyes may not yet behold Him. And in those very moments, Mary is like the moon above us — steady, gentle, and faithful — guiding our steps until dawn returns.

She does not replace Christ. She leads us to Him.

She does not stand between us and the Lord. She walks beside us toward Him.

To stay close to Mary is to stay close to the One she reflects.

And the more we welcome Christ as she did, the more *we* will shine His light into the world.

Closing Prayer

Lord Jesus, You are the Light of the world.
Teach me to rest my heart in You as Mary did.
Let her example of faith, humility, and trust be my guide,
especially when the path feels dim.

Mary, Mother of God,
reflect the light of Christ into my life,
and lead me always to your Son.

Amen.

When the Light Breaks In

There has always been fear in the human heart. We fear what threatens us from the outside — instability, conflict, uncertainty. But the deeper fear, the quieter fear, is the one that rises from within: the fear of being changed.

Archbishop Fulton Sheen reminds us that when Christ came into the world, He came like a **burst of light** — not to destroy, but to reveal. His arrival caused a *fallout* of grace, forgiveness, mercy, and new life. Hearts were awakened. Souls were stirred. Lives that had been wandering suddenly found their true path.

Tax collectors became honest.
Shepherds became brothers of a King.
Those who searched the heavens discovered the Lord of Heaven itself.

But light does not only show what is beautiful.
It also shows what we try to hide.

And so, some resisted the Light.
Some tried to push it away.
Some put up the old sign: **No Room.**

Not because they hated God, but because they feared change. They feared what might have to be surrendered, released, or confessed.

Yet look at the ones who were not afraid:

- The **shepherds**, who knew their poverty and ran toward the Light.
- The **Wise Men**, who let a star guide them more than power or politics.
- A **young woman**, who said Yes without knowing the cost.
- A **humble carpenter**, who trusted God more than appearances.

They entered the cave — the first shelter of grace — and found peace.

The Light still shines.
The fallout still falls.

It is not the destruction of life, but the rebirth of it.

And the only choice we must make is this:

Will we hide from the Light — or walk toward it?

May we find His presence today, even in the places we least expect.

The Life That Spreads Like Light

———————

Grace is not simply a teaching or a memory.
It is a **life** that flows from Christ to us.

Just as warmth spreads from fire,
or fragrance from a flower,
so the life of God spreads to those who draw near Him.

Christ became man so that God's own life
could pass into ours.

To be a Christian, then, is not only to admire Him —
but to **receive Him**.

The more we stay close to Christ —
in prayer, in silence, in charity —
the more His life becomes our own.

If we come near enough,
we will begin to love with His love.

A Love That Stoops

God's love does not remain distant.
It bends, it lowers, it stoops — all the way to a cradle of straw.

We often imagine that we must climb our way to God —
through effort, virtue, achievement, or strength.
But Christmas tells us: **God comes down to us**.

He comes not to overwhelm us, but to meet us where we are.
He chooses simplicity so that no one is intimidated.
He chooses littleness so that no one is afraid.

The God who stoops to us invites us to stoop to one another
— to serve, to forgive, to listen, to love.

May we find His presence today, even in the places we least expect.

Lord Jesus, grant me the grace to love You more today than yesterday, and more tomorrow than today.

Amen.

The Gift of Adoration

———————

When the Wise Men reached Bethlehem, they did not **ask** for anything.

They **offered** something: their worship.

True love does not begin with "What can I receive?"
It begins with "What can I give?"

Adoration is not flattery or obligation — it is the heart recognizing the One for whom it was made.

Kneeling is not humiliation — it is **freedom,**
because the soul bows only to the One worthy of worship.

The Wise Men teach us that the greatest gifts we bring to Christ are not gold or treasures — but **our hearts made humble in love**.

May we find His presence today, even in the places we least expect.

Lord Jesus, grant me the grace to love You more today than yesterday, and more tomorrow than today.

Amen.

The Grace of Being Found Where We Are

When the angels came with the announcement of Christ's birth, they did not go to the palace, the temple, or the wealthy households of influence. They appeared instead to shepherds — men who lived quietly, worked faithfully, and were rarely noticed by the world. They were simply doing their job when heaven opened.

God comes to us the same way.

We do not need to be extraordinary for God to draw near. We do not need to wait for life to become peaceful, impressive, or spiritually ideal. God comes to us while we are in the middle of our responsibilities — our work, our parenting, our caregiving, our daily routines, our hidden sacrifices.

The shepherds were not seeking visions, yet God found them.

They were not trying to make history, yet history walked into their lives.

The lesson is simple and liberating:

Holiness begins right where we are.

When we are faithful to the small things entrusted to us — the tasks no one sees, the kindness no one applauds, the burdens we carry quietly — our hearts become *a place where God can speak.*

It is not our position that prepares us for grace.

It is our **faithfulness.**

Remain where God has placed you.
Stand watch in the field entrusted to you.
Do your work with love — and heaven will find you there.

Prayer

Lord Jesus,
Teach me to be faithful in the ordinary duties of my life.
Give me a shepherd's heart — steady, humble, and attentive.
When You come, may You find me where I am supposed to be,
serving with love and listening for Your voice.

Amen.

The Sign of Smallness

If we were to imagine how God would enter the world, we might picture glory, brilliance, and overwhelming majesty. Something unmistakable. Something impossible to ignore.

But the sign that God gives us at Christmas is the *opposite* of what we expect:

A Child.
Wrapped in bands of cloth.
Lying in a manger.

God does not overwhelm — He invites.

He does not frighten — He draws near.

He does not force our love — He allows Himself to be held.

In becoming small, Christ makes Himself *approachable*.

There is no one too broken, too poor, too exhausted, or too ashamed to come close to a child.

God knows that our hearts often close when we feel confronted or judged.

So He comes to us in the gentlest form possible — so that **no one is afraid to come near Him.**

He takes on the limits of our humanity:

- He knows hunger.
- He knows cold.
- He knows loneliness.
- He knows tears.

So that when we say, *"Lord, do You understand?"*
He can answer, *"Yes — I have lived it."*

The manger is not merely a scene of sweetness.
It is a declaration:

There is no part of the human condition into which God will not enter in order to save us.

The sign of Christmas is not power, not majesty, not overwhelming light.

The sign of Christmas is *smallness*.
A God who becomes touchable.
A God who can be held.
A God who wants to be close.

Prayer

Lord Jesus,
You came to us in humility and tenderness.
Teach me to recognize Your presence in what seems small and unremarkable.
Give me the courage to draw near to You,
and the grace to receive the love that You offer.

Amen.

The God Who Took on Our Life

When St. John writes, *"The Word became flesh,"* he is announcing something so astonishing that we can spend our entire lives contemplating it and never exhaust its meaning.

The God who created the heavens and the earth
did not remain distant from His creation.

He entered it.

He took on a body that could grow tired,
a heart that could love,
a voice that could speak our language,
and eyes that could look into ours.

He became like us — in everything but sin —
so that we would never have to face life alone.

The Incarnation tells us that God does not save us from afar.
He steps into our story.
He takes our humanity to Himself — not temporarily, not symbolically, but fully and forever.

He knows hunger.
He knows tears.
He knows joy and friendship.
He knows betrayal and wounds.
He knows death.

Nothing in our humanity is foreign to Him now.

This means **we are not praying to a God who is unable to understand us.**
We are speaking to One who has walked the path we walk.

To say, *"The Word became flesh,"* is to say:

- God is not beyond our reach.
- God is not intimidated by our weakness.
- God is not disappointed by our humanity.

He chose it.

He embraced it.

He redeemed it.

Christmas is not simply the celebration of a birth.
It is the revelation of a God who says:

**"Your life matters to Me.
Your wounds matter to Me.
Your humanity is not something I despise —
it is something I came to save."**

Prayer

*Lord Jesus,
You who took on our human life,
draw close to me in mine.*

*Sanctify my joys, strengthen my sorrows,
and enter the ordinary places of my day.*

*May my heart never forget
that You know me from the inside —
and that You walk with me always.* **Amen.**

The Peace We Are Afraid to Receive

The angels sang *"Peace on earth"* at Bethlehem — but peace is more than silence, more than comfort, more than a passing feeling.

True peace is the harmony of a soul rightly ordered:
God above all,

the heart surrendered to His grace,
and love freely shared with others.

This peace is not achieved by effort alone.
It is received.

But we often resist it.

There is, in nearly every heart, a hidden room — a guarded place we refuse to open to God. A habit we will not surrender... a resentment we keep... a comfort we cling to... a wound we do not trust Him to heal. And so, we settle for a restless peace — the peace of managing life, instead of offering it.

Christmas is the reminder that God desires to dwell **with us** — *Emmanuel.*

The infinite God entered our world through simplicity, humility, and surrender.

He did not demand our strength — He asked for our hearts.

To give God our will is to allow Him to reorder our loves. To surrender the guarded place is to let His peace begin.

The Child of Bethlehem is the same Lord who gently says: *"If you give Me your heart, I will give you My peace."*

Closing Prayer

Lord Jesus,
You are Peace itself.
Teach me to trust You more than I trust myself.
Show me the place in my heart that I keep locked,
the place I fear to surrender.

Give me the courage to open that door to You.
May Your presence bring order, healing, and rest.
May Your love reshape my desires
until my heart becomes a home for You.

Jesus, I give You my heart.
Make it Yours.

Amen.

The Cave We Choose

There is a strange pattern in human history: when God's light draws near, the human heart must choose. It will either open — or retreat.

Archbishop Fulton Sheen reminds us that in Bethlehem, Christ was pushed into a cave because the world was too occupied, too self-assured, too crowded to receive Him. But now, centuries later, the cave returns again — not the cave that *held* Christ, but the cave *we choose* to hide in.

Today, we do not fear the **Light of God**, but the light of our own making — the forces, pressures, anxieties, and threats we have constructed with our own hands. The world retreats underground not only in fear of conflict, but in fear of truth, conscience, and conversion.

When we forget God, we begin to fear one another.
When we silence conscience, fear grows louder.
When we ignore grace, we run from the very One who can save us.

The true fear of God is not terror — it is love.
A child fears to wound the heart of a father who loves him.

But when love is forgotten, fear fills the void.

The angels said to the shepherds, **"Fear not."**
Not because the world was safe — but because **a Savior had come.**

Not merely a teacher.
Not merely an example.
A Savior.

The cave of Bethlehem is still open.
The Light still shines in the darkness.
But each heart must decide:

Do we push the Light away to protect our habits, our pride, our comfort —
or do we let Him enter the hidden places where we are most afraid?

Christ does not wait for the world to be calm.
He comes *into* the fear.
He comes *into* the cave.
He comes *for* us.

May we find His presence today, even in the places we least expect.

The Ones Who Kneel

———————

The first to find the Christ Child were not the powerful, the influential, or the self-assured. They were two groups who, though very different, shared something essential: **humility**.

The Shepherds came with empty hands.

The Wise Men came with full hands.

But both came with **open hearts**.

The Shepherds were the ones who *knew they knew nothing*.

Their lives were simple, their wisdom unpolished, their vision sharpened not by books but by quiet nights under the stars. They recognized the voice of God because they had learned to listen.

The Wise Men were the ones who *knew they did not know everything*.

They had searched the skies, studied the patterns of the universe, and discovered the limits of their own brilliance. Their learning led them not to pride, but to wonder.

Both knelt.

Christmas is never found by the proud.

Not by the self-satisfied.

Not by the one who believes he has no need of God.

Christmas is found by the searching heart—
the one hungry for meaning, longing for truth, ready to kneel.

The Shepherds did not understand everything, but they came.

The Wise Men did not see the whole road, but they followed the star.

Those who kneel will always find the Child.

May we find His presence today, even in the places we least expect.

The Doorway That Requires Us to Bend

———————

There is a profound truth hidden in the manger at Bethlehem:

You cannot enter unless you are willing to bend.

If a proud man were to step into the stable—full of opinions, full of accomplishments, full of himself—he would likely see nothing but poverty and insignificance. He would see straw, not a throne. Silence, not wisdom. A helpless infant, not the God of the universe.

Pride blinds us—not because God hides, but because pride refuses to kneel.

To the proud, the angels seem foolish, the shepherds naïve, the Wise Men misguided. Mary becomes just another mother. Joseph becomes merely a carpenter. And the Child becomes only a child.

But to the humble, everything is radiant.

The shepherds saw glory because they knew they needed saving. The Wise Men saw God because they knew they did not know everything.

Mary saw the face of Love because her heart was empty enough to receive Him.

To enter Bethlehem, we must stoop.
To see God, we must become small.
To find the Child, we must become like a child.

The miracle of Christmas is not that God became little—
but that He invites us to become little too.

And the moment we kneel, the cave becomes a cathedral,
the straw becomes a throne,
the silence becomes a song,
and the Child becomes our King.

May we bow low enough to see Him.
May we find His presence today, even in the places we least
expect.

The God Who Bent Low

———————

It is difficult to fathom the humility of God taking on our humanity.

Archbishop Fulton Sheen invites us to imagine something almost unthinkable:

If a human soul were placed into the body of a serpent — retaining full human awareness while limited to the movements, instincts, and sounds of a creature far beneath him — that would be humiliation.

But that would *still* be nothing
compared to what God embraced in the Incarnation.

For the Eternal Word took on the limitations of a human body — hunger, fatigue, cold nights, hard roads, misunderstanding, mockery, betrayal.

The Wisdom of God chose to speak in human syllables.
The One who fashioned galaxies
worked with calloused hands beside fishermen
who did not yet understand Him.

This lowering — this **bending down** — began in Bethlehem,
when the God who holds the stars
was held in the arms of a mother.

And it continued to the Cross,
where love went to its deepest depth.

No Crib without the Cross.
No Straw without the Nails.

The manger is only tender because the Cross is true.
The Child came not simply to be among us,
but to **save us** —
to enter our condition all the way down
so that we could rise all the way up.

If we struggle to imagine living as something beneath us,
how much more should we marvel
at the God who chose to live among us.

He bent low,
so we could be lifted high.

May we find His presence today,
even in the places we least expect.

The Cradle and the Cross

————————

The wood of the manger
and the wood of the Cross
come from the same tree of love.

Christ accepted the stable at His birth
because hearts had no room for Him.

He accepted the Cross at His death
for the very same reason.

From the beginning,
He came to give Himself completely.

There is no tragedy in His life —
only purpose,
only love freely offered.

For those who know themselves to be stables —
places poor, humble, and in need —
His coming brings joy.

For where He is welcomed,
everything is made new.

PART IV

MARY & JOSEPH
The Holy Home. Hidden Love.
Ordinary Holiness.

"Mary kept all these things, pondering them in her heart."

— Luke 2:19

INTRODUCTION

To love Christ is to enter the **home of Nazareth**.
There we meet Mary — full of grace, silent and strong — and
Joseph — steadfast, obedient, hidden.

Nazareth was not a place of miracles and wonders, but of daily
love lived faithfully. It is the school where God learned to
speak, to work, to obey, to love.

Mary teaches us to receive Christ; Joseph teaches us to guard
Him. Mary shows us tenderness; Joseph shows us courage.
Both show us that holiness is often hidden and unnoticed.

To dwell with them is to let our hearts be formed in love.

In Nazareth, love was lived quietly.
There were no crowds, no miracles, no speeches —
just daily faithfulness.

Mary and Joseph teach us
that holiness grows in ordinary days.
In simple work.
In patience.
In gentleness.

When we make room for Christ in the hidden places of life,
He grows within us.

Let us learn from the Holy Family
how to love in silence
and to be faithful in small things.

Christmas: The Mother Resembles the Child

When a child is born, we look to see whom the child resembles.
But at Christmas, everything is reversed.

Christ did not come to resemble Mary.
Mary came to resemble Christ.

She was not the source of His holiness —
He was the source of hers.

Archbishop Fulton Sheen reminds us that Mary did not simply give Christ His physical life.

Christ first gave her the fullness of grace, so that she could be a fitting home for Him.

Her purity, her humility, her tenderness — these were reflections of the One she carried.

And here is the great paradox:
Mothers often lift their children's eyes upward and say, "Heaven is above."

But when Mary held the Child in her arms,
she looked down to Heaven.

Christmas reveals a love that changes us from within.
The closer we draw to Christ, the more we resemble Him.

This is the true meaning of devotion to Mary —
not to stop at her, but to learn from her
how to hold Christ, how to love Him, how to resemble Him.

May we welcome Him in the quiet places of our hearts.
May we find His presence today, even in the places we least
expect.

To Make Room for the Gift

So often we live beneath the life God wants to give us.

We settle for:

- what feels safe,
- what is familiar,
- what we think we can manage on our own.

We tell ourselves to "try harder,"
to "be better,"
to "do more."

But Christmas does not say, *Try harder to reach God.*
Christmas says, *God has come to you.*

The spiritual life begins not with effort,
but with **receptivity**.

A heart open to God can receive more than it can imagine.
A heart closed — even slightly — cannot receive at all.

Grace does not overwhelm us.
It waits to be welcomed.

The Christ Child comes small and gentle.
so that He can be received.

But to receive Him, we must make room —
not room in our schedule,
not room in our intellect,
but room in our **heart**.

We fear that if we give God too much, He will take more than
we are ready to surrender.
But the truth is simpler:

**We give Him our little —
and He gives us His everything.**

We offer our spark —
and He offers His flame.

We offer our weakness —
and He offers His strength.

We offer our finite heart —
and He pours His infinite love into it.

We become more not by pushing ourselves higher,
but by opening ourselves wider.

This is the meaning of Bethlehem —
God entering our littleness.

And this is the invitation of Christmas —
to receive Him.

Prayer

Lord Jesus,
Make my heart open.
Help me to receive the love You desire to give me.
Free me from the fear of surrender.
Teach me to trust that You do not diminish me —
You complete me.

Take my spark,
and give me Your flame. **Amen.**

The House of Bread

Bethlehem means **"House of Bread."**
And the Child born there called Himself **the Bread of Life.**

He comes to feed the hunger that lies deeper than the body —
the hunger of the soul.

We can fill our days with activity, noise, experience, success,
and yet still feel a quiet emptiness within.

This hunger is holy.
It is the heart recognizing its need for God.

The manger is a table.
The Child is the Gift.

To receive Him is to be fed with life that does not fade.

May we find His presence today, even in the places we least expect.

*Lord Jesus, grant me the grace to love You more today than yesterday, and
more tomorrow than today.*

Amen.

The Silence of Mary

————————

Mary speaks little in the Gospels —
not because she has nothing to say,
but because love is often expressed best in **silence**.

In silence, she received the angel's message.
In silence, she carried God within her.
In silence, she stood by the Cross.

Silence is not emptiness —
it is space where God can speak.

If we fill our lives with noise —
constant movement, constant demands, constant distraction —
we may miss the whisper of God.

Mary teaches us a different way:

- to listen,
- to wait,
- to trust,
- to ponder.

Her silence is not withdrawal;
it is **communion**.

May we find His presence today, even in the places we least expect.

Lord Jesus, grant me the grace to love You more today than yesterday, and more tomorrow than today. **Amen.**

The Hidden Years

Most of Christ's life was hidden — quiet, ordinary, unseen.

No crowds.
No miracles.
No public teaching.

Just love — lived faithfully, day by day.

This tells us something profound:
Holiness is not found only in extraordinary moments.
It is found in **the ordinary**, offered to God.

The home, the workplace, the conversations we repeat,
the duties we carry — these are places where love can grow.

Bethlehem leads to Nazareth.
The wonder of Christmas leads to the simplicity of daily life.

God is not far from our routine.
He is *in* it.

May we find His presence today, even in the places we least expect.

Lord Jesus, grant me the grace to love You more today than yesterday, and more tomorrow than today.

Amen.

The Joy That Comes from Surrender

———————

Mary did not choose the easy path.
She chose the **true** one.

Her "Yes" carried weight:
misunderstanding,
uncertainty,
poverty,
sacrifice.

Yet her soul **rejoiced**.

Joy does not come from comfort or convenience.
Joy comes from **saying yes to God**,
even when we do not see the full picture.

We may not know where the path leads —
but if we walk it with Him,
it will always lead to joy.

May we find His presence today, even in the places we least expect.

Lord Jesus, grant me the grace to love You more today than yesterday, and more tomorrow than today.

Amen.

The Peace That Comes When We Surrender

———————

Peace is not simply quiet or stillness. Even thieves at rest in their hiding place may be calm. True peace is something deeper — it is the harmony that comes when **everything in us is ordered rightly**:
God above all,
the soul governing the body,
love guiding all our desires.

This is why the angels sang *"Peace on earth"* at the birth of Christ. They were announcing not the end of worldly conflict, but the beginning of **a new order of the heart**.

Yet we often miss the very peace we long for.
We ask to be healed, but not changed.
We ask to be saved, but not from our favorite sins.
We want to belong to God — but on our own terms.

Deep within every soul, there is a **small guarded garden**, a place we keep locked and hidden.
It holds the one thing we refuse to surrender —
the habit we cling to,
the attachment we excuse,
the relationship we won't purify,
the fear we refuse to confront.

And as long as we keep that garden to ourselves, peace cannot enter.

At Christmas, Mary gave Christ His human nature.
She held nothing back.
And God, receiving everything, gave everything in return.

So it is with us.
If we surrender our guarded garden,
if we give Him our will — the only gift that is truly ours —
our hearts become the second Bethlehem:
a place where God is **with us,**
not distant or remembered,
but living and present.

Christ is **Emmanuel** — God with us.
With us in weakness.
With us in the ordinary.
With us in what we cannot fix or understand.
He does not wait for us to be strong.
He comes to us *because we are not.*

And when we open our hearts to Him,
even a little,
He brings the peace that the world cannot give —
the peace that flows from **union with the One who loves us.**

A Quiet Prayer

Lord Jesus,
You are the peace my heart was made for.
Take from me the one thing I cling to,
and give me the courage to surrender my will to Yours.
Be born in me anew this day,
that I may live in Your peace,
and share it with others. ***Amen.***

The Poverty of God

Christ chose poverty — not because poverty is comfortable, but because **love desires nothing to separate it from the beloved**.

By becoming poor, Christ removed every barrier between Himself and us.

He became accessible, touchable, approachable.

No throne separates us from Him.

No magnificence overwhelms us.

No greatness frightens us.

He comes to us needing — so that we will not fear needing Him.

The poverty of Bethlehem is the language of love:
I come close so you may come close.

May we find His presence today, even in the places we least expect.

Lord Jesus, grant me the grace to love You more today than yesterday, and more tomorrow than today.

Amen.

Mary, the First Monstrance

Before Christ was lifted in the monstrance upon the altar,
He was lifted in the arms of His Mother.

Mary was the first to **carry Him**,
the first to **adore Him**,
the first to **offer Him** to the world.

Her whole life was a silent Eucharist:

- She received Him.
- She loved Him.
- She gave Him.

When we gaze upon Christ in the Eucharist,
we are invited to love Him as she did —
with a heart that is quiet, trusting, and full.

To love Mary does not take us away from Jesus —
it places us beside Him.

May we find His presence today, even in the places we least expect.

Lord Jesus, grant me the grace to love You more today than yesterday, and more tomorrow than today.

Amen.

The Handmaid of the Lord

Mary called herself the **Handmaid of the Lord** —
the one who serves.

Her greatness is not in power,
position,
accomplishment,
or recognition.

Her greatness is in **availability**.

God does not need our strength.
He needs our **yes**.

Mary teaches us that holiness is not achieved —
it is **received**,
by allowing God to lead.

When we surrender our plans,
He gives us His peace.

May we find His presence today, even in the places we least expect.

Lord Jesus, grant me the grace to love You more today than yesterday, and more tomorrow than today.

Amen.

The Gift We Can Hold

If the world were already whole, Christ would not have come. The manger does not tell us that humanity has reached greatness — it tells us that humanity *needs to be healed.*

Christ comes not because we are strong, but because we are broken.

He comes not because our love is complete, but because our hearts are aching for something more — something steady, enduring, real.

Every human heart longs to love something it can truly hold. We try to embrace ideas, movements, causes, and dreams — but they cannot hold us back.

We try to cling to success, comfort, admiration, or accomplishment — but these slip through our fingers like sand.

Our hearts were made to love someone we can draw close to.

And so God does something astonishing:

He becomes small.

The God who spoke galaxies into being
chooses to be held in human arms.

The Eternal enters time.
The Infinite becomes touchable.
The All-Powerful becomes vulnerable.

Not to prove a point —
but to give us permission to love Him.

He comes to make an exchange with us —
an exchange no one else could ever offer:

- Our need for His fullness
- Our wounds, for His healing
- Our sorrow, for His joy
- Our emptiness, for His life
- Our humanity, for **His** divinity

The manger is not sentimental.
It is an act of divine generosity.

Christ does not wait for us to become worthy.
He comes to make us whole.

He comes so that **love may finally have somewhere to rest.**

Prayer

Lord Jesus,
You know the hunger of my heart.
and the longing that lives within me.
Teach me to bring You my weakness,
my limits,
my need —
so that I may receive Your strength,
Your grace,
Your love.

You became small so that I could draw near.
Draw near to me now. ***Amen.***

The Garden Where God Chose to Dwell

When God prepares to do something extraordinary, He does not rush. He works in patience, in symbol, in silence, and in love.

Before the Word became flesh, the longing for Him echoed through prophets, covenants, and signs: a burning bush that blazed but was not consumed, a flowering staff in the quiet of the sanctuary, an ark that held the very law of God. These were hints — glimpses — of something greater to come.

But symbols were not enough.

God desired a dwelling place that was not only foretold, but *formed*.

So He prepared a paradise — not of rivers and fruit and earthly beauty, but of grace, humility, and purity. A garden not planted in soil, but in the heart of a woman.

Mary is that garden.
The place where heaven found a home.
The sanctuary where God breathed His life into our humanity.

In her, the Divine and the human are no longer separated.
In her, God begins His journey toward us.
In her, the world receives not just a promise, but a Person.

And just as God prepared Mary to welcome Christ, He prepares us too — patiently, quietly, gently.

He asks only this:
that we make room,
that we listen,
that we allow grace to grow.

For the miracle of the Incarnation does not end in Bethlehem
— it continues wherever Christ is welcomed.

May we allow our hearts to become a garden of His presence.
May we find His presence today, even in the places we least
expect.

The Door by Which He Came

Christ did not come to us in lightning, power, or display.
He came through a woman.

God chose to be carried, to be sheltered, to be held.

He entrusted Himself to a Mother — not because He needed
her, but because **we** did.

Mary is not an obstacle to Christ.
She is the *way* Christ chose to come.

If God wished, He could have appeared full-grown and radiant.
But instead, He came small enough to be welcomed,
humble enough to be received,
close enough to be touched.

And He came through her.

This is why the Church calls Mary the *Gate of Heaven.*
Not because she replaces Christ,
but because she is the door He passed through —
and the one we pass through when we come to Him.

To refuse Mary is not to reject a devotion.
It is to refuse the way God wanted to be known.

She formed Him once in her womb.
She forms Him still in the hearts of those who invite her.

Where Mary is, Christ draws near.

Where Mary is welcomed, faith becomes warm, personal, and alive.

For she is the Mother who teaches us how to love Him.

May we invite her again — gently, simply, sincerely —
into our prayer,
our home,
our heart.

So that Christ may once more be born in us.

May we find His presence today, even in the places we least expect.

The Dream of God

Every love story begins long before two hearts ever meet.
There is a desire, a longing, a quiet vision of what love could be.

So it was with God.

Before Mary ever walked the earth,
before there were mothers, cradles, lullabies,
before Bethlehem, Nazareth, or Galilee —
she lived in the heart of God.

She was the dream of God's love,
the masterpiece imagined before the gallery existed.

There were two images God held for each of us:
the person we are,
and the person we were meant to be.
And most of us live somewhere between those two pictures.

But in Mary, the dream and the reality were one.

What God desired, she became.
What God envisioned, she lived.
The music written in heaven was played perfectly on earth.

She is humanity without its fractures,
love without the wound,
purity without the fear of being misunderstood.

She is the one in whom God's longing was answered.

And because of her, Love Himself could take flesh.

We do not lose Christ by loving Mary.

We find Him where He first learned to love.

If we let her draw near,
our hearts too may begin to look like the heart that God
dreamed for us.

May we find His presence today, even in the places we least
expect.

If You Could Choose Your Mother

Imagine, for a moment, that you existed before your own mother.

Imagine that you could shape her — her character, her tenderness, her heart — the way an artist shapes a masterpiece.

Would you choose anything less than the best?

Would you choose a mother who embarrassed you, who was selfish, who lacked purity or kindness?

Or would you desire one whose very presence lifted your soul — a woman gentle in speech, rich in compassion, strong in quiet dignity, beautiful not just outwardly, but in the deeper beauty of holiness?

If *we*, with limited love and imperfect wisdom, would want the best of mothers…

How much more would Christ?

Christ did not simply arrive in the world and *accept* whatever mother He happened to have.

He *chose* her.

He chose a mother whose heart would be completely open to God.

A mother unstained by sin, unbroken by selfishness, unshadowed by pride.

A mother whose love was so pure that He, the Author of Love, could rest in it.

Mary is not an obstacle to Christ —
she is the door He chose to enter by.

And Archbishop Fulton Sheen tells us something poignant:

If you want to know the heart of a man, look at how he treats his mother.

If you want to know the heart of a faith, look at how it speaks of the Mother of Jesus.

To honor Mary is to honor Christ's own choice.
To draw close to her is to draw close to the One who fashioned her for Himself — and for us.

May we welcome her,
that the love of Christ may be born again in us.

May we find His presence today,
even in the places we least expect.

Love Comes from Heaven

In most families, a child begins with the love of two hearts.

There is tenderness, desire, and hope — and yet, even this love is fragile and limited.

Parents can long for a child, but life always arrives as mystery.

But the Birth of Christ was different.

Here, love did not rise from earth to heaven — **it came from heaven to earth**.

Mary did not simply discover life within her.
She *willed* to receive the Life of God:

"Be it done unto me according to Thy word."

Her motherhood began not in the body, but in the heart.

The Holy Spirit overshadowed her,
and in that holy surrender, **Love became Flesh.**

This is what Christmas reveals:

Love is not only something God gives.
Love is Who God is.

And when Love takes flesh,
Child and Love become one.

May that same Love be born in us —
quietly, simply, wherever there is room.

113

PART V

THE BETHLEHEM WITHIN
The Birth of Christ in the Soul.
Union. Love that lives.

"That Christ may dwell in your hearts through faith."

— Ephesians 3:17

INTRODUCTION

There comes a moment when the story of Bethlehem must move from **memory** to **reality** — from something we admire to something we live. Christ desires not only to be adored in a manger, but to be **born in the soul**. This is the deepest mystery of the Christian life: *Christ in you, the hope of glory.*

The outward story has led us inward.

The Child who once lay in a cradle now asks to dwell in the heart.

This final section is not about looking at Christ — but allowing Him to **live in us**.

Christ was born in Bethlehem once, but He desires to be born in us again.

This is the deepest meaning of Christmas — that the Child who lay in the manger now seeks a home in the heart.

We do not force this.
We simply say yes.
We welcome Him.
We stay near Him.
We let love do its work.

When Christ lives in us,
our lives become a light for others.

Let us open our hearts
and allow Him to be born within.

Let Christ Be Born in You

We celebrate Christmas as a historical event — Christ born in Bethlehem.

But Archbishop Fulton Sheen reminds us that the greater miracle is Christ born **in the soul**.

It is possible to admire the Nativity and yet never experience the **new birth** it offers.

It is possible to know *about* Christ and still never *welcome* Him.

God waits to be invited.

As Mary freely gave her *yes*, we too are asked to open our lives to the life of God — gently, honestly, humbly.

Christmas happens whenever we say:
Lord, come. Be born in me.

May we find His presence today, even in the places we least expect.

Lord Jesus, grant me the grace to love You more today than yesterday, and more tomorrow than today.

Amen.

The Bethlehem Within

There are, in truth, **two births of Christ.** One happened long ago in Bethlehem, in a stable under the quiet sweep of the stars. The other must happen **in the human heart.** We remember the first with carols and nativity scenes, but the second is the one that changes us. The Babe of Bethlehem came **not only to be born in a manger,** but to be born **in us.**

Other great figures in history—Caesar, Napoleon, Lincoln, Buddha—have influenced minds and movements, but **none of them can be born within souls.** Christ alone enters the world **and** enters the person. His coming divides history, and His coming into our hearts divides our lives: *before* and *after* grace.

But His birth stirs resistance. Just as Herod feared the Child in Bethlehem, so there is something in us that hesitates to surrender—an ego that does not want to yield, a will that fears to be transformed. Yet the birth of Christ in the soul does not destroy us; it **fulfills** us. It gives us a new way of valuing, choosing, loving, and hoping.

This is what St. Paul prayed for when he wrote to the Ephesians, longing that Christ might **"dwell in your hearts by faith"** and that they be **"rooted and grounded in love."**

He knew that the greatest miracle of Christmas is not only that God once came to earth—
but that He continues to come.

119

Bethlehem is not far away.
It is nearer than we think.
It is as close as the moment we say:

"Come, Lord Jesus. Be born in me."

May we welcome Him today,
and discover **the Bethlehem within**.

The Jesus We Choose

There are many versions of Christ spoken about in the world.

Some are sentimental; some are political; some are merely historical. There are countless retellings, reinterpretations, and reimaginings. But not all of these are the Christ who was born in Bethlehem.

C. S. Lewis once imagined a devil teaching another devil how to tempt souls. His advice was simple: *Do not remove Christ entirely. Instead, change Him.* Let Him be admired—but not obeyed. Discussed—but not followed. Praised—but not surrendered to.

The enemy does not fear a Jesus who stays in the past.
He fears the Christ who lives in the heart.

The danger of every age is the temptation to create Christ in our image—one who blesses our preferences, echoes our desires, and never contradicts us. A "safe" Christ. A Christ who makes no demands.

But the real Christ calls us to conversion.
He calls us to holiness, honesty, sacrifice, and love.

He is not merely a teacher of gentle wisdom. He is the Savior who enters our sin to redeem us. He is the Lamb who takes away the sins of the world. He is the God who comes not to affirm us as we are, but to make us new.

The question at Christmas is not *Do we believe in Jesus?*
The question is: **Which Jesus do we believe in?**

The Christ we *make* leaves us unchanged.
The Christ who *comes* changes everything.

May we welcome the living Christ—
the One who saves, the One who heals,
the One who loves us too deeply to leave us as we are.

May we find His presence today, even in the places we least expect.

When God Feels Far Away

There are seasons when God seems distant —
not absent, but hidden.

We ache for Him.
We long for Him.
We remember a closeness we once knew.

This longing is not a failure of faith —
it is faith in its most honest and tender form.

We do not grieve what we do not love.

The heart that laments God's hiddenness
is a heart in which God already dwells.

Sometimes the nearness of God is too deep for feelings.
Sometimes He comes to us disguised in silence.

If we continue to seek Him,
even longing becomes prayer.

May we find His presence today, even in the places we least expect.

Lord Jesus, grant me the grace to love You more today than yesterday, and more tomorrow than today.

Amen.

The Divine Infection

Grace is not merely a lesson or an idea —
it is **a living life** shared by God.

Just as a flame lights another flame without losing its brightness,
Christ shares His life with us.

If we stay close to Him —
in prayer, in silence, in sacraments, in love —
we begin to live with His strength,
His peace,
His compassion.

To be Christian is not only to admire Jesus,
but to **receive His life**
until His love becomes our own.

May we find His presence today, even in the places we least expect.

Lord Jesus, grant me the grace to love You more today than yesterday, and more tomorrow than today.

Amen.

The Hidden God

For nine months, God was hidden in Mary.
For thirty years, God was hidden in Nazareth.
For centuries, God is hidden in the Eucharist.

God often works **quietly**,
patiently,
gently.

We want miracles, flashes, signs.
But God often moves in the slow growth of love.

Do not mistake **quiet** for **absence**.

The hidden God is the faithful God.
The God who dwells, stays, abides.

Holiness is not spectacular —
it is steady.

May we find His presence today, even in the places we least expect.

Lord Jesus, grant me the grace to love You more today than yesterday, and more tomorrow than today.

Amen.

The Son of God, Our Brother

———————

Christ did not only come to save us —
He came to **stand with us.**

He knows our hunger,
our fear,
our laughter,
our sorrow.

He is not ashamed to call us His brothers and sisters.

Let us not treat Him as a distant figure,
but as One who walks beside us.

We belong to Him.
We are family.

May we find His presence today, even in the places we least expect.

Lord Jesus, grant me the grace to love You more today than yesterday, and more tomorrow than today.

Amen.

To Call God Father

There are moments in life when God can seem distant.
Prayer feels quiet.
Faith feels abstract.
The heart wonders: *Does God truly know me? Does He see me? Does He care?*

Christmas answers those questions.

God does not remain far away.
He steps into our world.
He takes on our humanity.
He places Himself in our arms.

He becomes a Child
so that we may become children of God.

This is not poetry — it is the deepest truth of our faith:

In Christ, we do not simply worship God — we belong to Him.
We do not merely follow Him — we are His sons and daughters.

And just as a child does not earn a parent's love,
we do not earn God's.

We received it.

Like any child growing up in a family, we learn slowly.
We make mistakes, fall, and begin again.

But in every season, the Father is the One who holds us, forms us, and calls us His own.

This is why Jesus teaches us to say:

"Our Father."

Not *Creator, Almighty, Distant One, Mystery Beyond Reach* — though He is all of these.

But **Father.**

Someone who knows us.
Someone who wants us.
Someone who loves us.

To know God as Father is to live life not as an orphan, but as one who is held.

We do not walk alone.
We walk with the One who calls us His children.

Prayer

Father,
You have claimed me as Your own through Your Son.
Teach my heart to rest in Your love.
Remove whatever keeps me from trusting You.
Let Your love shape my thoughts,
my choices,
my life.

Jesus, my Brother,
help me to live as a child of God.

Amen.

Becoming Who We Are Called to Be

———————

The world often tells us what it thinks we are:

- A collection of impulses.
- A bundle of needs.
- A life driven by instinct, desire, and self-preservation.

But Christmas tells a different story.

When God takes on our humanity, He reveals something profound about us:

We were made for more than survival.
We were made for love.

We are not accidents of nature.
We are not merely bodies that think.
We are not defined by our failures or weaknesses.

We are created in the image of God.

And when we look upon Christ, the Child in the manger,
the Teacher who walks among us,
the Saviour on the Cross,
the Lord risen in glory —
we see who we are meant to become.

In Him we recognize:

- Our potential for wisdom beyond our instincts.
- Our capacity to choose what is right over what is easy.

- Our calling to love even when love demands sacrifice.

We begin to understand that the transformation God desires for us.
is not about becoming *less human,*
but about becoming **fully human** —
as God intended from the beginning.

This is the *higher evolution*:

Not the evolution of bodies,
but the evolution of the **heart.**

The path is not pride, but surrender.
Not self-confidence, but confidence in God.
Not self-exaltation, but self-giving love.

It begins with a simple prayer:

"Lord, make me what You created me to be."

A prayer of trust.
A prayer of humility.
A prayer of becoming.

Prayer

Lord Jesus,
When I look at You, I see the person I am called to become.
Give me the courage to follow You.
Give me the humility to be changed by Your love.
Help me to surrender what is small in me.
so that Your greatness may grow in me.

I am Yours.
Form me into the person You created me to be. **Amen.**

The Greatness of Being Small

How do we truly find God? We often imagine that we must climb toward Him—through knowledge, strength, achievement, or accomplishment. But the mystery of Christmas reverses the direction. The infinite God comes down to us, and He comes *small*.

In the natural world, a child sees greatness everywhere. To the little, everything is large: a father seems mightier than all men, a hill becomes a mountain, and even a beanstalk reaches the stars. It is only when we grow *bigger* in our own eyes that everything else begins to seem small.

So too in the spiritual life.

There is a connection between **childhood** and **humility**. We cannot always remain physically small, but we can become *small of heart*. We can choose the simplicity that recognizes how great God is, and how much we need Him. Humility is not humiliation—it is clarity. It is seeing ourselves as we are and God as He is.

When we magnify our own ego—when self becomes the center—there is no room left for wonder. But when we become little, when we surrender our pride and self-sufficiency, then the greatness of God reveals itself again. The soul that bends low becomes able to look high.

Christmas is the reminder that the infinite God can be found in the littlest of forms:

a Child in a manger,
a whisper in prayer,
a hidden grace received quietly.

To find the God who became small, we must become small ourselves. Not insignificant—but open, receptive, trusting—as a child.

The one who kneels sees the stars more clearly.

When the Heart Misses God

There are seasons when God feels distant—not gone, but hidden. The soul hungers and thirsts for something it can no longer touch, and the ache becomes its own form of prayer.

We do not mourn what we do not love.

We do not feel absence unless Presence once mattered.

There is a loneliness that comes from having known God, having tasted grace, having once been held close by the warmth of faith. The one who has loved deeply grieves more profoundly when love seems silent.

But this longing is not a failure of faith.
It *is* faith—waiting in the dark.

The soul that aches for God already belongs to Him. The pain is the proof. The yearning is the evidence. The emptiness is not the absence of God, but the space He is preparing to fill.

Christ does not avoid the places where we feel most alone.
He draws near there—quietly, gently, like a Child laid close to the heart.

When we cannot feel Him, He is often nearest.

When we cannot see Him, He may be standing just beyond the veil of our sorrow.

When we ache for Him, it is because His love has already claimed us.

The longing is not the end of faith.
It is the doorway to encounter.

May we find His presence today, even in the places we least expect.

The Bread Our Souls Hunger For

Bethlehem means *House of Bread*.

And there, in that quiet village, the Bread of Life was laid in a manger— a place where creatures feed.

It is as if God were saying:

"You hunger—but not only in the body.
Come, and I will feed your soul."

We spend so much of life feeding our outward needs—work, comfort, entertainment, success—yet the deeper hunger remains. The heart longs for meaning, belonging, forgiveness, love, and peace. No earthly bread can satisfy that longing.

Christ did not come to be a king of stomachs, or a distributor of earthly goods. He came to nourish the inner life. He came to satisfy the hunger beneath all hungers.

Those who have tried to fill their souls with the pleasures of the world eventually discover how thin such food is. The soul becomes weary from eating what cannot nourish it.

But Christ comes to Bethlehem—
not in power, but in simplicity,
not to overwhelm, but to offer Himself.

He is Bread for the journey,
Strength for the weak,

Peace for the restless,
Love for the lonely.

Our deepest hunger is not for something,
but for Someone.

**May we come to the manger in simplicity and truth,
and find the Bread our souls have always longed for.**

May we find His presence today, even in the places we least
expect.

The Brother Who Knows Our Hearts

Christ is **God with us** —
but He is also **God like us**.

He knew hunger and weariness,
joy and sorrow,
laughter and tears.

There is no pain you can feel
that He has not carried in some way.
No loneliness He has not known.
No burden He has not shared.

He is not ashamed to call us His brothers and sisters.

The only question is whether we will treat Him
as family —
or only as a distant acquaintance.

He waits for a place in our daily lives,
not just our Sunday prayers.

PART VI

TREASURY OF CHRISTMAS MEDITATIONS
For Prayer and Reflection Throughout the Season

"And she gave birth to her firstborn Son ... and laid Him in a manger.

— Luke 2:7

INTRODUCTION

There are seasons when the grace of God gathers in one place, like light pooling in a quiet corner of the soul. Part VI is such a place.

Throughout this book, we have walked the familiar paths of Advent, Christmas, Epiphany, the Holy Family, and the Bethlehem within. Yet the mystery of Christ's coming is too rich to be contained in neat divisions. Some reflections rise in unexpected moments. Some insights come as gentle sparks long after the feast. Some meditations ask not for a chapter of their own, but for a home where they can simply shine.

This final part is a **treasury** — a collection of meditations offered for any day, any moment, any place in the season where the heart desires a word of grace.

Here you will find thoughts born of prayer, lines that invite deeper stillness, and reminders of the God who walks among us. They do not follow a sequence because grace does not always move in order. They do not belong to one theme because Christ belongs to every moment. They are given so that your heart may have something to reach for — in joy, in longing, in quiet evenings, or in the early dawn when the world is still waking to the mystery of Christmas.

Let these meditations meet you wherever you are.
Use them as your prayer.
Carry them into your Holy Hour.
Return to the ones that speak softly and stay.

For Christ comes not only in the great feasts, but in the hidden moments of reflection. Not only in the liturgy, but in the quiet stirring of the heart. Not only in Bethlehem long ago, but **now**, wherever you open a little space for Him.

May this treasury help you receive the grace that continues to spread through the season —
the grace of the God who came near,
who remains with us,
and who invites us to welcome Him again and again.

Come, Lord Jesus.
Be the light that fills every corner.

Do Not Settle for a "Safe" Jesus

The world is comfortable speaking about Jesus as a teacher, a figure of history, a symbol of kindness — because such a Jesus asks little.

But the real Christ calls us to holiness.

He asks for our hearts, our decisions, our conversion.

A Christ who only inspires us but does not transform us is not the Christ of Bethlehem.

He comes not to be admired — **but to be followed.**

Not to remain outside of us — **but to dwell within us.**

Let us not settle for the Christ of sentiment, when the living Christ stands before us, calling us by name.

May we find His presence today, even in the places we least expect.

Lord Jesus, grant me the grace to love You more today than yesterday, and more tomorrow than today.

Amen.

Christ for Every Season of Life

There is a quiet wisdom in the way God comes to us.

He does not ask us to be older or wiser or holier than we are.

He meets us exactly where we stand — at the age we are, in the season we are living, with the questions we carry right now.

The young find in Christ **promise** —
a vision that calls them to something greater than themselves.

Those in mid-life find in Christ **purpose** —
a steadying presence that guides decisions, responsibilities, and the work entrusted to them.

The elderly find in Christ **peace** —
a gentle light that gathers the years into meaning.

Christ does not wait for us to reach a particular stage to reveal Himself.

He knows the longings of every age of the human heart:

- The young long for direction.
- The adult longs for strength.
- The elderly long for rest.

And Christ is all of these:

The Way.
The Strength.
The Rest.

But there is something even deeper:

Though Christ meets each of us personally, we see Him most clearly *when we come to Him together.*

Faith is not just individual — it is shared.
The Child in the manger gathers all of us — young and old, searching and steady, hopeful and weary — into one family.

To approach Christ together is to discover:

The Christ who understands us personally
Is the same Christ who unites us as one.

The manger is not only a cradle.
It is a meeting place.

Prayer

Lord Jesus,
You know the season of life I am in.
Meet me here —
in my questions, in my work, in my longings.

Teach me to recognize You
as the One who guides, strengthens, and consoles.

And draw us together as Your family,
so that we may see You more clearly
and love You more deeply.

Amen.

When Fear Drives Us into Our Caves

Archbishop Fulton Sheen tells us that every age has its cave —
the place where humanity hides from God.

In our time, the cave may not be made of stone,
but of distractions, noise, self-reliance, and guarded hearts.

We fear silence because silence reveals the soul.
We fear stillness because stillness invites God.

But Christ does not wait for us to emerge strong.
He enters the cave **with us**.

The Child of Bethlehem comes not to condemn our fear,
but to banish it with love.

We do not have to be brave to welcome Him.
We only have to be willing.

May we find His presence today, even in the places we least expect.

Lord Jesus, grant me the grace to love You more today than yesterday, and more tomorrow than today.

Amen.

God Walked Our Earth

The universe is vast —
full of stars, galaxies, and mysteries we cannot measure.

Yet God chose **our** small world.
He walked our roads, breathed our air,
felt fatigue, hunger, joy, loneliness, and hope.

Every religion tells the story of humanity seeking God.
Christmas tells the story of **God seeking humanity**.

Not from afar,
but up close.

The Creator placed His feet
upon the dust He Himself had formed.

The One who made the stars
walked beneath them.

He did not come to overwhelm us,
but to draw near enough
for us to love Him.

God walked our earth —
and He walks it still
where hearts make room.

May we find His presence today, even in the places we least expect. Lord Jesus, grant me the grace to love You more today than yesterday, and more tomorrow than today. **Amen.**

His Name Shall Be Jesus

The Name **Jesus** is not simply a label —
it is a mission.

It means: **God saves.**

Just as Joshua once led God's people
into the promised land,
Jesus leads us into the promise of eternal life.

Every time we speak His Name with love,
we call upon the One who:

seeks,
forgives,
heals,
and saves.

The simplest prayer in the world
is also the greatest:

Jesus.

May we find His presence today, even in the places we least expect.

Lord Jesus, grant me the grace to love You more today than yesterday, and more tomorrow than today.

Amen.

It's Free

We cannot lift ourselves to God.
So God came down to us.

Grace is not earned.
It is received.
It is **gift**.

But love never forces.
It invites.

When we surrender —
even a little —
God lifts us more than we could lift ourselves in a lifetime.

To give Him your heart
is to discover what freedom truly is.

May we find His presence today, even in the places we least expect.

Lord Jesus, grant me the grace to love You more today than yesterday, and more tomorrow than today.

Amen.

Where Is He Who Is Born King?

Every soul longs for a king —
someone worthy of love, loyalty, and trust.

But the King who comes at Christmas
does not demand a throne.

He enters quietly.
He reigns in humility.
He comes not to rule over us,
but to dwell within us.

To find Him,
we do not look to power or applause —
but to silence, simplicity, and love.

May we find His presence today, even in the places we least expect.

Lord Jesus, grant me the grace to love You more today than yesterday, and more tomorrow than today.

Amen.

The Cradle Points Towards the Cross

———————

The wood of the crib
and the wood of the Cross
are part of the same story.

Christ came not only to be born,
but to pour Himself out in love.

From the beginning,
the Cross was already in His Heart.

Christmas looks forward to Good Friday —
and both reveal a love that never stops giving.

May we find His presence today, even in the places we least expect.

Lord Jesus, grant me the grace to love You more today than yesterday, and more tomorrow than today.

Amen.

Those Who Found Him

On the night of Christ's birth,
only two kinds of people recognized Him:

The shepherds —
the simple of heart,
who knew they knew nothing,
and were therefore open to wonder.

The wise men —
the truly learned,
who had discovered that no matter how much they knew,
there was still mystery beyond their reach.

Both humility and wisdom
bowed before Christ.

Pride did not kneel at Bethlehem.
Self-certainty did not travel to the manger.
The comfortable and complacent did not hear angels sing.

But those who were willing to be small,
or willing to keep searching,
found Him.

Christmas invites us to return to that place:

the quiet of trust,
the honesty of need,
the reverent openness of the heart.

If we seek Him with humility,
we will find Him —
just as they did.

May we find His presence today, even in the places we least expect.

Lord Jesus, grant me the grace to love You more today than yesterday, and more tomorrow than today.

Amen.

Loved First

_____

We sometimes live as though we must earn God's love — as if holiness is a ladder and God waits at the top to see whether we have climbed high enough. But the mystery of Christmas teaches us something very different. We did not climb to God.

God came down to us.

Before we ever thought of Him, He thought of us.

Before we knew how to love, **He loved us.**

Before we took our first breath, **He chose us.**

Christ comes in the flesh to reveal a truth we could never discover on our own:

We are loved not because of our goodness, but because of His goodness.

When a child begins to recognize a mother's love, the love is not new — the awareness is. The love was present long before the child could understand it. So it is with God. His love has surrounded us from the beginning. We only slowly awaken to it.

If we believe God loves us only when we are strong, holy, or successful, then we will spend our lives hiding our weaknesses from Him.

But if we believe God loves us *because He is love*, then even our weakness becomes a place where grace can enter.

The Christian life does not begin with trying to love God. It begins with **allowing ourselves to be loved by God.**

Everything follows from that.

Prayer

Lord Jesus,
Help me to rest in the truth that Your love comes first.
Free me from striving to earn what You have already given.
Open my heart to receive Your love more deeply,
so that I may become who You created me to be.

Amen.

A Love That Gives Itself

We live in a world that uses the word "love" often, but rarely understands it.

Love is spoken of in songs, celebrated in movies, and claimed in promises — yet so much of what is called love today is simply desire, emotion, or attraction.

True love does not ask, *"What can I receive?"*
True love asks, *"What can I give?"*

Love that seeks only pleasure burns brightly and then disappears.

Love that pours itself out endures — because it is rooted in sacrifice.

At Bethlehem, we see this clearly.
The Christ Child does not come to *take*, but to *give* —
His entire life is a gift poured out.
Even the manger speaks of this gift: the wood that cradles Him now, will one day support Him on Calvary.

The cradle and the Cross are made of the same wood.

Love always gives itself.

And standing beside this mystery is St. Joseph —
quiet, strong, watchful, faithful.

His love for Mary is not possessive, demanding, or self-centred.
It is protective.

It is reverent.
It is pure.

Joseph loved with a strength that did not need to grasp or control.
His love was deep enough to be selfless.

This is the kind of love our hearts are made for —
a love that honours the other,
a love that protects what is holy,
a love that reflects Christ Himself.

At Christmas, Christ teaches us how to love:
not by reaching upward in desire,
but by bending low in service.

And Joseph shows us how to live that love every day.

Prayer

Lord Jesus,
Teach me to love as You love —
not by seeking my own gain,
but by giving myself for the good of others.

St. Joseph, guardian of purity and protector of the Holy Family,
help me to love with a strong, patient, and selfless heart.

May the wood of the manger and the wood of the Cross
shape my love into a gift.

Amen.

The Grace of Seeing Through

A sense of humour, in the deepest spiritual sense, is not merely the ability to laugh.

It is the gift of *seeing through* the surface of things —
seeing meaning where others see only circumstance.

It is easy in life to become weighed down by what feels heavy:

- responsibilities,
- disappointments,
- frustrations,
- and the constant demands of daily living.

When we forget that God is present in all things,
life begins to feel closed in and overly serious,
as if everything depends entirely on us.

But grace gives the soul lightness.
Grace teaches us how to look again — and to see differently.

To have a "spiritual sense of humour" is to recognize:

- that sorrow does not have the final word,
- that darkness does not have the final say,
- that God is quietly at work, even when hidden.

The saints could smile in times of suffering.
not because they enjoyed the trial,
but because they *saw beyond it.*

They looked *through* their difficulty.
and recognized the God who was there —
guiding, transforming, redeeming.

Christmas restores this vision.

The Child in the manger looks like weakness — yet it is infinite love.

The stable looks like poverty — yet it contains the Lord of Heaven.

The Cross looks like defeat — yet it is victory.

To believe this is to recover the grace of joy.

It is to say:

I do not need to see everything clearly —
I only need to trust the One who is here.

One day, when our journey is complete,
the first sight that will make heaven *heaven*
will be the smile of Christ — the One we have been learning to
see through the veil of this world all along.

Prayer

Lord Jesus,
Give me the grace to see You in all things.
Lighten my heart when I grow weighed down.
Teach me to look beyond appearances.
and to recognize Your loving presence
even in the ordinary and the difficult.

May my faith become a quiet joy,
and may I learn to rest in Your smile. **Amen.**

Do Not Delay the Visit of Love

———————

There is an old story told among the Russian people of a woman known as Baboushka. One winter night, as she tended her home, the Wise Men passed by on their pilgrimage to Bethlehem. They had seen the star and were hurrying to worship the Child whose birth had stirred heaven and earth.

"Come with us," they invited.

But Baboushka looked around at her work — the hearth to tend, the house to order, the tasks she felt she *could not* leave undone.

"I will come," she said, "but not yet. When my work is finished, I will follow and find Him."

But *her work was never finished.*

By the time she stepped outside, the star had faded from the sky, and the travelers were far beyond her reach. She sought the Child, but the moment of encounter had passed her by.

Yet the story does not end in sorrow.

For though she missed the first call, she continued to seek Him in another way. Believing that the Christ Child might now be found in any little one who is cold, hungry, or alone, she began to care for every child she met. And so, on Christmas mornings, the tradition says she still travels from home to home, giving gifts of warmth and tenderness — searching for the One she once delayed in greeting.

There is a Baboushka in every human heart.

We, too, intend to give ourselves to Christ — but *later*.

When life settles.

When things are less busy.

When the house is in order.

When we feel more ready to be holy.

We forget that Love does not wait for our perfection — only for our *yes*.

Christ does not reproach our hesitations. He simply continues to arrive — hidden in the poor, in the weary, in the unnoticed, in the small opportunities to love that pass before our door each day. Every act of mercy, every kindness given without return, every gentle word spoken when it would be easier to remain indifferent — these are the places where Christ appears again, still seeking to be welcomed.

The invitation of Christmas is simple:

Do not delay the visit of Love.

Do not let the tasks of life make you miss the One who is Life.

Do not wait for better conditions to begin to love.

For Christ is nearer than we imagine — and waits only to be recognized.

God Walked Where We Walk

———————

The world is vast.
The stars are uncountable.
The universe overwhelms our smallness.

And yet — the greatest wonder is not in the heavens,
but in the truth that **God walked our earth.**

He breathed our air.
He worked with our hands.
He knew hunger, weariness, friendship, joy, and sorrow.

Other religions tell of humanity searching for God.
Christmas tells of **God searching for humanity.**

He came not in thunder or flame,
but with human feet on familiar ground.

The One who made the stars
walked beneath them.

The One who holds all things in existence
let Himself be held.

He did not come to overwhelm us —
He came to be loved.

And He remains where hearts make room.

May we seek Him with reverence,
and welcome Him with tenderness.

The Footsteps of God

―――――――――

Sometimes we are reminded how small our earth is — a tiny speck in a vast universe. Yet its greatness lies not in its size, but in what happened upon it.

God walked here.

The One who scattered galaxies and shaped the stars chose to enter our world as a child. He breathed our air. He walked our roads. He touched our sorrow. He knew our hunger and our hope.

We are not merely searching for God.
God has searched for us.

He came not to dazzle us with power, but to draw near with love —
to be held, to be known, to be welcomed.

And He still walks our earth —
in every act of mercy,
in every humble offering,
in every heart that makes room for Him.

May we find His presence today, even in the places we least expect.

The Name That Saves

———————

There are many names in the world, but only one given for our salvation.

Jesus.

A name that does not merely *identify* Him — it *reveals* Him.

In the Old Testament, Joshua led God's people into the Promised Land.
In the New Testament, **Jesus** leads us into eternal life.

To speak His Name is to remember:
God has not abandoned us.
He has come for us.
He has come *to save.*

Sometimes prayer fails us — the heart is heavy, the words are few.

But the Name remains:

Jesus.
In temptation — *Jesus.*
In sorrow — *Jesus.*
In gratitude — *Jesus.*
In dying — *Jesus.*

This Name is not far from us.
It is near to the lips,
near to the heart,
near to the one who calls.

It is the Name spoken by shepherds in wonder,
by sinners in hope,
by saints in love.

Let us speak His Name with tenderness,
with trust,
with longing.

For every time we whisper it,
He draws near.

**May we find His presence today, even in the places we
least expect.**

The Grace That Spreads

Not all infections are harmful.
Some heal. Some restore. Some give life.

Christmas is the beginning of such an infection.
God entered our humanity so that His life could pass into ours.

C.S. Lewis once imagined a child wondering if a toy soldier
could ever become alive.

That is what happened at Christmas:
the Divine took on our nature—not as play, but as love.

And because humanity is not a collection of isolated souls,
but a single living family across time,
when Christ took our flesh,
He touched *all of us*.

Grace began to move through the human race like warmth
through cold limbs,
like spring thawing a frozen field.

But a gift given to all must still be **received** personally.
The life of Christ does not overwhelm us — it invites us.
We "catch" it by drawing near to Him.

We catch His patience
by spending time with Him.
We learn His mercy
by letting Him forgive us.

We receive His strength
by leaning on Him when we are weak.

The closer we come to Him,
the more His life becomes ours.

**Christmas is not only God with us.
It is God *within* us.**

May we find His presence today,
even in the places we least expect.

The Gift That Cannot Be Earned

We cannot lift ourselves to God by effort alone.
No matter how hard we try,
our strength is too small,
our understanding too narrow,
our resolve too fragile.

So God came down.

If humanity could not rise to heaven,
Heaven chose to kneel beside us.

Just as a man must reach down to lift a flower,
God stooped down to lift our nature into His life.
But He did not force His way in —
He waited for a free yes.
And Mary gave it.

In the same way, grace waits at the door of our hearts.
God does not seize us.
He invites.

To receive Him is not to lose ourselves,
but to become our truest selves.
It means letting Love shape what is wounded,
letting Light enter what is dim,
letting Peace reach where fear has lived too long.

The gift is free.
But love, when freely given,
changes everything.

We fear that if we give God an inch,
He will take our whole life.
And He will.
But not to diminish it —
to make it radiant.

To be held by Love is not captivity.
It is freedom.

And this is Christmas:
God offers Himself —
and waits for our yes.

May we find His presence today,
even in the places we least expect.

He Took Our Nature, So We Could Take His

———————

The Gospel does not say,
"God became an idea."
It says,
"The Word became Flesh."

God did not come to theorize about humanity.
He came to **live it**.

There is **no sorrow**, no confusion, no loneliness,
no hunger of the body or hunger of the heart
that He did not choose to enter.

He is Brother to the one who suffers quietly.
Brother to the restless young soul searching for identity.
Brother to the forgotten prisoner.
Brother to the one hiding tears behind laughter.
Brother to the one who doubts, who rebels, who fears.

There is not a single human heart
He did not come to meet.

We often speak of the "fall of Adam,"
but Archbishop Fulton Sheen reminds us to ask:
Is the wound of Adam stronger than the healing of Christ?
If we inherit the brokenness of the first man,
shall we not also share
in the **restoring love** of the second?

We are not distant relatives of God.
Not strangers tolerated at the edge of the family.

We are His kin.
His brothers.
His sisters.
His beloved.

From the cry of the Child in Bethlehem
to the cry from the Cross on Calvary,
the message is the same:

"I am not ashamed to be one of you.
Come, be one with Me."

May we find His presence today,
even in the places we least expect.

The Humility of God

———————

To help us imagine the humility of the Incarnation,
Archbishop Fulton Sheen asks us to picture what it would be
like to become a creature far below us,
to live among it,
to speak its limited language.

And then he tells us:

This is **only the faintest** comparison
to what God did for us.

The Child in the manger already bears within Him
the shadow of the Cross.
The humility that began in Bethlehem
is fulfilled on Calvary.

Love bends low —
so low that nothing is beneath it.

That is the love that saves the world.

About the Author

ALLAN SMITH is a Catholic evangelist, radio host, and spiritual director who has spent over a decade proclaiming the wisdom of Archbishop Fulton J. Sheen to audiences around the world. As the founder of Bishop Sheen Today, Al has edited and published dozens of classic Sheen titles, including 'The Cries of Jesus from the Cross' and 'Lord, Teach Us to Pray'.

A passionate promoter of Eucharistic Reparation and devotion to the Holy Face of Jesus, Al regularly speaks at parish missions, leads retreats, and hosts weekly radio broadcasts across Canada, the United States, Ireland, Australia and the Philippines. His work has helped reintroduce Sheen's powerful spiritual legacy to a new generation.

He lives in Canada with his family and continues his mission of calling souls to deeper intimacy with Christ through the example of saints like St. Thérèse of Lisieux and the timeless teachings of Fulton J. Sheen.

To learn more or to access free devotional resources, visit our two websites at:

www.bishopsheentoday.com
www.holyfacemiracle.com

A Personal Invitation

Over the years, I have had the privilege of helping souls draw closer to Christ through prayer, silence, and the beautiful wisdom of Archbishop Fulton J. Sheen. If this devotional has nourished your heart, you may also find these works helpful in your journey of faith.

✷

Advent and Christmas with Archbishop Fulton J. Sheen

A Devotional Journey of Waiting, Welcoming, and Living the Mystery

✷

The Holy Face and the Little Way

A Spiritual Friendship with Christ, St. Thérèse, and the Holy Face

✷

Behold Your Mother

Mary, the Cross, and the Power of Reparation

The Cross and the Last Words

A Journey Through Calvary with Fulton J. Sheen

✵

Lord, Show Us Thy Face and We Shall Be Saved

A Mission of Light, Truth, and Eucharistic Renewal

✵

Priest, Prophet & King

Meditations on Identity, Mission, and the Call to Holiness

✵

The Sheen Mission Series — Collected Meditations

Over 100 of the Richest Reflections from Retreats, Radio, and Prayer

✵

May every book you read be an open door to the heart of Christ.

May these works draw you deeper into
prayer, trust, peace, and surrender.

And may the Child of Bethlehem be born again in you.

Come, Lord Jesus.

www.bishopsheentoday.com

www.ingramcontent.com/pod-product-compliance
Lightning Source LLC
Chambersburg PA
CBHW072021060426
42449CB00033B/1354